The Power of Sensitivity

Success Stories by Highly Sensitive People
Thriving in a Non-sensitive World

TED ZEFF, Ph.D.

FOREWORD BY ELAINE ARON, Ph.D.
AUTHOR OF *THE HIGHLY SENSITIVE PERSON*

Publisher's Note

This publication is designed to provide accurate and authoritative information in regard to the subject matter covered. It is sold with the understanding that the publisher is not engaged in rendering psychological, financial, legal, or other professional services. If expert assistance or counseling is needed, the services of a competent professional should be sought.

Copyright © 2015 by Ted Zeff
Prana Publishing
P.O. Box 84
San Ramon, CA 94583

Cover and interior design by Megan Jones Design
Edited by Teja Watson

ISBN 978-0-9660745-4-3

Prana Publishing

First Printing

Other Books by Ted Zeff

The Highly Sensitive Person's Survival Guide

The Highly Sensitive Person's Companion

The Strong Sensitive Boy

Raise an Emotionally Healthy Boy

Contents

Foreword

I am so happy to introduce this book to you. I read it in one afternoon, with many other things to do, saying to myself "just one more story" until I had finished it, utterly satisfied. This book is a lovely gift to all highly sensitive people.

There are three major reasons for my hearty recommendation of this book. First, in it you will meet other highly sensitive people—reading it is very much like going to an HSP (highly sensitive person) Gathering Retreat or other event that is "all-HSP." With only HSP voices, the effect builds and builds: *This trait is real; I am not alone.*

Second, while I expected and read some "outer" success stories, the majority were about inner successes: of healing, of changing ways of thinking, and of speaking the truth that sometimes only a highly sensitive person can see. Sometimes the breakthroughs were small, at least by some external criteria, but they made a great difference to these HSPs and those around them. And these HSPs know that these introspective and private stories are the real successes in life.

Third, I found it a pleasure that this book, probably quite unintentionally, demonstrates how each HSP is different—in history and even in temperament traits—yet we have something underlying that is the same. Highly sensitive people have these four facets in common: (1) thinking deeply; (2) being easily overstimulated; (3) feeling emotions, pain, and empathy so intensely; and (4) noticing subtleties others miss. These are all facets of the same gem.

The only disadvantage to being an HSP, which comes up again and again and must be dealt with, is that we are easily overwhelmed by all the stimuli in the world, bombarding us as we try to stay attuned to these depths. That is simply part of the package.

So many of the stories in this book are about speaking up, and *seeing this as a success.* That is truly a reason for pride and hope. The world so desperately needs those who observe, reflect, and then speak up with both passion and logic. That is the formula for a better world, and the formula is inherent in the inborn survival strategy of HSPs. Sometimes we are wrong and need to process that, too. But usually, at the very least, we are bringing up something that others have not thought of. Because of the technological powers of our species, this consideration of all sides of an issue is essential for the well-being not only of humans, but of the entire living world.

Enjoy the book!

—Elaine N. Aron, Ph.D.

Acknowledgments

I am so grateful to Elaine Aron for all her support and encouragement in writing this book as well as for her continued research, writing, and speaking, which have helped millions of highly sensitive people throughout the world. I greatly appreciate all the highly sensitive people who have shared their inspiring success stories—which will help many other HSPs (highly sensitive people) thrive in our frequently less-than-friendly non-HSP world. I want to especially thank Mary Pavitra Foster for suggesting the topic of this book. I am so thankful to my spiritual teacher, Amma, whose compassion and love have inspired millions of people to serve humanity and find inner peace.

Introduction

A highly sensitive person is someone who is aware of subtleties in their surroundings and is easily overwhelmed when they are exposed to a highly stimulating environment. Highly sensitive people make up 20 percent of the population in every country, and the trait is equally divided between males and females.

The HSP may find it challenging to screen out stimuli and can be easily overwhelmed by noise, crowds, and time pressures. The HSP tends to be very sensitive to pain, the effects of caffeine, and violent images. Highly sensitive people may also be made extremely uncomfortable by bright lights, strong scents, and changes in their lives.

The highly sensitive person has a finely tuned nervous system and is adversely affected by a fast-paced and aggressive society. HSPs tend to process sensory stimuli more deeply than most people. It can be both an enjoyable and a challenging trait to have.

Even if you feel that you only have some of the characteristics of a highly sensitive person, but those qualities are extremely true for you, you may still consider yourself an HSP. Regardless of whether you consider yourself to be very sensitive or only slightly sensitive, the information in this book will be valuable for you.

Many HSPs have experienced low self-esteem when told that they are flawed for being different, or have experienced anxiety and tension when interacting with loud, aggressive people or being exposed to constant stimuli throughout the day.

In this book, *The Power of Sensitivity*, many inspirational HSP success stories are presented that will motivate you to thrive at an optimal level. As you read the uplifting success stories, you will come to appreciate your trait of high sensitivity and understand how beneficial it is to be an HSP.

The book contains 43 success stories that have been submitted from sensitive people from 10 different countries. Highly sensitive people throughout the world have shared their triumphs and happiness, living with the trait of high sensitivity—and I have gathered them here to empower the global HSP community.

The contributors in this book utilized their innate gifts as HSPs to overcome the challenges of living in a Non-HSP world. These highly sensitive people used many of the following inborn, positive traits to flourish in our aggressive, overstimulating world:

- Creativity
- Intuition
- Spirituality
- Strong sense of justice
- Conscientiousness
- Loyalty
- Appreciation of beauty, art, and music

- Awareness of potential danger
- Create positive changes in the environment
- Kindness
- Compassion
- Enthusiasm for life

How to Use This Book

There are 25 different sections, arranged alphabetically so you may easily find what you are most interested in reading about. However, I think all the stories have information that is valuable for the highly sensitive person.

You will read about how HSPs have successfully dealt with career challenges, and how learning about and accepting the trait of high sensitivity has positively transformed their lives. Many practical techniques for raising sensitive children are presented by parents, and stories about the unique challenges and opportunities of sensitive men are included here as well.

Also, various self-care methods are offered, such as the benefits of tuning into the body and engaging in somatic healing techniques, as well as various forms of alternative healing, like intuitive healing and innovative sound programs. Some of the other HSP-empowering stories include areas of medical care, diet, relationships, speaking up, sleep, travel, dealing with noise, and coping with tragedy.

After each uplifting story, I have included additional information on how to integrate that story's success into your life. After reading each story, you may want to sit quietly and contemplate whether the methods presented in the story could also benefit your life as a sensitive person. Then spend a few minutes thinking about, and possibly writing down, how you can incorporate the new techniques into your life.

Sharing some of the helpful stories with a close friend or partner is an excellent way to receive support for implementing the positive changes you desire. You may even want to put the new techniques on your calendar, or put reminders in your phone. At the end of the book is a list of resources for highly sensitive people.

This book is not only for highly sensitive people. Non-HSPs will benefit from reading this book, by learning how to support their HSP friends and relatives as well as learning new coping strategies for themselves.

Let's now begin reading these inspiring success stories by highly sensitive people from around the world—and move toward creating a planet full of empowered HSPs. By incorporating some of the techniques that have been so successful for other HSPs into your life, you too will become a successful, happy, and empowered highly sensitive person!

Chapter 1

Career and the HSP

Success at Work, the HSP Way

I come from a wonderful family of outgoing, confident people. They are excellent networkers, professionally highly successful, popular dinner party guests, and the life and soul of any party. I love them very much, yet I am completely unlike them.

Social situations have always been very challenging for me. The thought of attending a social event used to make me ill. I couldn't deal with the noise, the intensity of so many people, and it was emotionally excruciating for me to partake in small talk, especially since I thought that people were judging me (which at times was true). Over the years I've been told that I am nervous, overly anxious, and high-strung. I've been constantly told by others not to worry so much, not to be so shy, and to be more relaxed.

I surmised at a young age that the path to happiness for me lay in being completely other than I was, so I became very good at pretending, especially in a professional context. While adopting a faux persona during difficult times may be a valid choice, it is also exhausting. I simply couldn't keep faking it all the time, so I had to limit many new opportunities in my life.

I have worked in organizational development in various educational, media, and corporate industries. In my jobs, I wouldn't speak up, even to share my thoughts and ideas, or state my unhappiness with certain situations. I also wouldn't volunteer for new opportunities for fear that I would not be able to cope. In our age of high-powered networking, I would fabricate stories (actually lie) to avoid situations where I would have to meet new people. One strategy I employed was to arrive at networking functions late enough to avoid having to talk to anyone since the speaker had already begun speaking.

Sometimes, after a long day of pretending to be someone else, I could barely make it home. I would lie down in the peace and silence of my own home and wonder what was wrong with me. However, one day I was researching the trait of sensitivity on the Internet and found the work of Elaine Aron. I finally learned, at the age of forty-four, that there is nothing wrong with me! I am a highly sensitive person, and I can be myself and still thrive in my work environment.

Since learning about the trait of high sensitivity, I have integrated several key practices into my work life that have resulted in amazingly successful results. I have learned how to network in a way that works for me. I pick one person to talk to when I arrive at an event, and then include other people who I see standing alone. I also choose to listen more than I talk, thereby lessening expectations as to how I should behave. If I meet one interesting person at an event, I feel that I have been success-ful, and I make sure to later email them to let them know how much I enjoyed meeting them. I find emailing is far less stressful for me than calling someone, since I can prepare carefully in advance what I would like to say.

After one year of my new and improved networking I was elected president of my local human resources group. A col-league recommended me because I am "so good with people." I'm now feeling so confident that I regularly speak at many indus-try groups and university classes. Although I still become ner-vous before a speaking engagement, I'm able to follow through. I would never have agreed to give speeches before I learned how to approach my job from an HSP-friendly perspective.

I have also made many changes in my work life. I now work part-time, so I'm better able to balance the stimulation of the workplace with my less-stimulating home life. In the past I felt like I had little respite from the emotional storms my sensitivity created, but armed with my new HSP knowledge, I have ensured that I have clear boundaries in my working relationships and have effectively negotiated my way through office politics. I also now hold a senior position as manager of staff operations within a new warm and supportive work environment.

Finally, I am always honest with others about my need for time by myself and now live in a peaceful, natural setting on an island here in New Zealand. I feel restored by living in a natural and tranquil environment and I have actually introduced some elements of my peaceful home environment into my office set-ting. I am able to respectfully and honestly decline invitations if

I am feeling overstimulated or tired and have gratefully found that most people are accepting and understanding of my HSP-friendly lifestyle. My friends know that when I spend time with them, I really want to see them.

I've gone from feeling like a victim to becoming an empowered highly sensitive person.

—ANONYMOUS

The writer's inspiring story illustrates how important it is for HSPs to live with integrity and speak their truth. When we feel ashamed of who we are and pretend to be someone else, it creates additional stress and shame in our lives.

Unfortunately, if we've been constantly told that there's something wrong with us for being sensitive, we may not feel that we have a right to express our needs. Although it may be difficult at first to speak up and let others know what our needs are, stating what we want is essential for the HSP to feel inner peace and thrive. You may want to role-play with a friend, family member, or a counselor, expressing your needs in various situations until you start feeling comfortable doing it.

I'm impressed with the way the writer assessed their lifestyle and made the necessary adjustments, to live a more balanced life by working part-time and moving to a rural, natural environment. If you are working in a very stressful job that can't be modified, examine why you continue to work in a difficult situation. Investigate new job possibilities that are better suited to your temperament. Remember that sensitive people tend to work best in a quiet, calm, and supportive environment. And don't forget that HSPs need to accept their work limitations and not compare themselves with their non-HSP colleagues.

Finding a Job That Suits My Sensitive Temperament

In my mid-forties, when I finally had some extra time to complete my college education, I chose to pursue a career in nursing. I was familiar with the health care environment from seeking help with my special needs child and I looked forward to earning more money as a nurse. Since I'm also a very caring, sensitive, and nurturing person, I thought it would be a perfect fit. I went to night school for my prerequisites and then attended a two-year nursing program at a community college.

It has been three years now since I graduated and passed the state exam to become a registered nurse. However, I have never worked as a nurse and probably won't work in the field of nursing. One reason is the local economy. Most hospitals are not hiring and there are many applicants for the few open nursing positions where I live. However, the main reason that I probably won't ever work as an RN is that I've realized that as a sensitive person, the work environment does not suit my temperament.

When completing my internships and student rotations, I learned that the actual time most nurses spend with patients is minimal. One-to-one contact and nurturing patients took a back seat to passing out medications and completing paperwork. I was slow in completing my assignments because I felt that patients should be informed about all the medications they were taking, and I did not feel supported by my supervisors and instructors around this. Some nurses were very difficult to work with and I had to endure their loud outbursts of anger.

As a hospital nurse I had no privacy or quiet time. I was always on the floor, and my "office" was my medication cart/computer that was in the hallway at all times. I was bombarded with frequent interruptions that interfered with my ability to focus on my duties. I missed being able to have a quiet lunch hour during which I could center myself. My lunch break was thirty minutes in a noisy cafeteria with my classmates or nurse mentor.

Through my internship and classes, I discovered that I loved learning, yet it seemed as if there was never enough time to deeply explore any one topic in depth. I also found that I was more successful studying by myself than in a group and I had one of the highest grade point averages in my class. Although I enjoyed my studies, I became very anxious if I had a deadline to meet.

The most important lesson I learned from nursing school was to appreciate the job I had prior to going to school. My former job, which I have returned to, has been ideal for my HSP temperament. I work in the peace and quiet of my own home for my self-employed husband, which is the perfect environment for an HSP. I answer calls from home, do all the book-keeping, taxes, payroll, etc. Although I encounter a lot of interruptions, I frequently only have to work part-time, and I work by myself and have the added nurturing advantage of being able to bring my dog!

Unfortunately, eight years ago I felt embarrassed by my lack of professional skills and small income and consequently went through a very difficult process to feel better about myself. I now accept my limitations and have learned to be true to myself instead of seeking accolades from others. By giving up the false dream of pursuing a successful career, I feel better physically and emotionally.

—ANONYMOUS

It's important to remember that every HSP is different and some HSPs may enjoy working in a hospital environment. However, most HSPs would likely find working in such an overstimulating hospital environment very difficult. As a matter of fact, I have a friend who is an HSP medical doctor, and although he completed his degree and works as a physician, he told me that attending medical school and completing his internship and residency programs was extremely difficult for him. However, he now has his own practice where he spends as much time as he needs with his patients, which suits his HSP temperament.

Although hospital nursing would likely be exhausting for most HSPs, other nursing jobs might be less stimulating, such as working in homecare (with only one patient), a small health clinic, occupational nursing in a small business environment with a focus on wellness, a doctor's office with a small practice, or working in a community health agency.

In our materialistic-oriented society, even HSPs may internalize the belief that making more money is worth even the negative effect on your physical, emotional and spiritual well-being. Once your basic needs have been met, you may sometimes still drive yourself to earn more and more money believing that external remuneration will bring happiness. But studies show that there is no correlation between happiness in life and increased income once your basic needs have been met.

HSP Intuition Saved a Life

In the fall of 2011, I stumbled upon an HSP questionnaire that changed my life. I scored high on Elaine Aron's HSP self-test and realized very quickly that I'm a high sensation seeking HSP. A high sensation seeker is someone who enjoys stimulating activities, taking risks, and can become easily bored. Although I have always known that I was different, I didn't know how to express my needs to others until I read *The Highly Sensitive Person* by Elaine Aron.

Just a few days after finishing the book, I encountered a situation at work that had a powerful effect on my life. I have worked as a nurse for more than 20 years, mostly in an intensive care unit or critical care. While I enjoy my job, it can be exhausting at times. Although I'm the type of nurse that thrives on the excitement of the high-paced intensive care unit, on my days off I lay on the couch watching movies to recover from all the overstimulation. My colleagues tease me, since my down-time is so different from most of their "adrenaline-seeking" behavior.

For seven years, I have been part of a team that works out of the ICU and gives direction to other medical teams concerned with a patient, which is a new method here in Canada. The job requires strong assessment and interpersonal skills, helping physician lead teams to consider other options and treatments for their patients. It's imperative to be careful not to offend or upset the other teams. If my job is done well, the entire team works efficiently to ensure patient safety, but if it's done poorly, it can create strained relationships and patient care can be compromised.

A few days after finishing Elaine Aron's book, our team had a female patient who had shortness of breath and exhibited some distress right after a valve surgery. The patient had no other health concerns and had been recovering nicely. However, one of the nurses was concerned that something had changed. After an evaluation and chest X-ray, our team felt that extra physiotherapy and perhaps a diuretic would help. Since it was a weekend, only the surgeon and his resident checked in on the patient. It was tempting to just sign the patient off our list and allow the surgical team to manage her. However, since I was mildly concerned but couldn't articulate why, I asked to keep the patient on our list.

As the day progressed, I checked on the patient often, and each time she just seemed worse. She was only comfortable lying on her right side. With the HSP questionnaire fresh in my mind (aware of subtleties in the environment), I found myself intuitively asking some simple, yet probing questions: "If her body was trying to tell me something what would it be? Why is a healthy 60-year-old woman unable to sit up? Why does she only lie on her right side? And why am I so worried about her?"

It took a bit more processing on my part that day, but as I sat in my office pondering it all, I thought to myself, *At the end of your shifts when it is time to go home, you always leave feeling peaceful, knowing you have done what you could to save or help someone. You don't have this peaceful feeling today. Why are you so worried about this patient? Perhaps you might be picking up on things others can't see yet? If you don't make a bit of noise on behalf of this woman, you won't forgive yourself.*

Although I had a slight fear of the lead surgeon if I intervened, after my inner dialogue, I knew that I might be her only chance for survival. I used my good communication skills to discuss the situation with one doctor, but he replied that the surgeon had already called him about the patient and the patient was being monitored so there was no need for a transfer to ICU. However, I couldn't let the situation rest, so I asked the resident what he thought. He asked me if he should take the portable ultrasound to her bedside to see if he could check the heart for tamponade (accumulation of blood or fluid in the pericardial sac around the heart). I told him that since the surgeon hadn't ordered the test we would have to perform the procedure without his consent.

I hate not being truthful, but I also knew that performing this procedure was possibly her only chance to survive. I'm not sure how I knew this so deeply but I did. The test validated my intuitive feeling and within 60 minutes the patient was taken to the operating room, where a huge clot of blood was removed from her heart. She made a full recovery. I was told later that she was only minutes away from her heart stopping and that if I hadn't done what I did, she would have died.

If I could do it all again, I would not be so scared of the reaction from the surgical team and would just kindly, but forcefully explain my concerns, knowing I could make myself heard. It was a good learning experience for me. Although the diagnosis didn't come to me initially, I now know that my keen observation skills and inner strength helped me see the situation from many levels and help navigate that patient through the system.

As you can imagine, the experience created a complete over-arousal of my nervous system that lasted about three days, and subsequently, I needed lots of sleep. On one level I was the hero of the unit as my story made the rounds, but I was struck by how close to death the patient had been. I felt honored that I was able to use my HSP gifts to help her. Since this incident I'm much more confident to state my observations clearly and realize that I might be able to see problems before others in order to get patients the help they need.

—ANONYMOUS

Although this high sensation seeking HSP worked in a hospital ICU unit, she also really needed her downtime to recuperate from all the stimulation from her job. What a great gift it is to be highly sensitive person as the nurse in this story illustrated when she used her intuition, awareness of subtleties in the environment and conscientiousness to save the life of a patient. Once we realize the advantages of our special talents as an HSP, we will be able to speak up more easily, to state what needs to be done in any given situation.

Being an HSP Made Me a Better Doctor

I'm a Swedish woman, born in 1949, who has just retired as a medical doctor and I currently work part-time in my profession. I'm also divorced, with two lovely grown-up children and three wonderful grandchildren, of which two are HSP boys. I'm currently a member of the Swedish HSP society.

My parents divorced when I was 10 years old, and although my parents remarried others, I never felt like I had a real family again. I was the "shy" and silent child who took care of my two younger brothers. I was not competitive and could play for hours using my imagination. I was an observer who was very seldom angry, and though I frequently felt fear and sadness, I also experienced a lot of joy, passion, and enthusiasm.

As a child, I felt like I wasn't normal and consequently experienced loneliness. However, I've always felt that I needed to be true to myself. I always asked a lot of questions and read many books to discover who I am. While growing up I was always interested in how the mind and body function. Therefore, it's been a blessing to have worked as a general practitioner medical doctor. Even though I don't feel comfortable in groups, meeting with patients on a one-to-one basis has never been a problem.

Instead of asking a patient "What is wrong?" I ask myself inwardly what the purpose of a patient's medical symptom is. I've learned that the body tries to tell us when something isn't in balance. Frequently, the symptoms increase until the patient listens to what is out of balance. It has been a real gift for me to be able to see each of my patients as unique and to intuitively understand what the body is trying to tell the patient about their lifestyle.

I've started to study photography in recent years, and I've noticed that photography reminds me of how I process things as an HSP and as a physician. I zoom in to details and then zoom out to get the big picture. However, this constant zooming in and out can be draining, so I need my downtime.

In recent stress research it was shown that it's especially stressful for women who take on too much responsibility without any personal time for themselves. I am very responsible by nature and very careful in my work as a doctor, so I reduce the stress by making sure I spend some time alone when I'm not working.

Learning that I am an HSP has helped me both professionally and personally. I can now look back at that shy, lonely 10 year-old girl I used to be with both respect and love. I wouldn't have been able to accept my sensitivity and understand the

gift it has been in my work as a doctor if it weren't for Elaine
Aron's work.

—Ia Staaf

*Dr. Ia Staaf has been able to use her inborn intuition to suc-
cessfully treat patients. If there were more HSP medical doctors
who also looked inwardly for guidance about what the body is
trying to tell the patient, rather than just treating symptoms, I
think there would be a quantum leap in healing.*

A Highly Sensitive Speaker

I recently discovered that I am an extrovert HSP, and on ques-
tionnaires I have scored very high on empathy. While having
the empathetic trait can have its challenges, it makes me a very
good teacher.

As a full time computer instructor for adults here in
Denmark, I was able to tune in to the psychological makeup of
each student immediately. After talking to the students, I knew
how I would have to present the material to be successful.

Because I was able to intuit each student's needs, I received
excellent evaluations. Because of my high degree of empathy as
an HSP, I was able to give all my students an excellent learning
experience, which validated my desire to do a good job.

However, after four years of teaching I decided to change
jobs, since it was very stressful trying to be successful teaching

classes everyday. I was exhausted at the end of each day and realized I needed a job that was more HSP-friendly.

At the time, an old friend told me that there were openings for speakers for meetings to help people on disability, which I started doing. During my presentations I share my successes as an HSP, which inspires my audience. Being an HSP high sensation seeker, I enjoy giving talks and feel that I have a lot to contribute. I have used my empathy to not only heal myself, but to tune in to the mood of my audience. Giving talks occasionally, instead of teaching every day, has helped me feel calmer and more energetic since I have more downtime. Fortunately, I'm in a financial position where I don't need to work full-time.

During the presentations, I really enjoy sharing the trait of high sensitivity. I recently shared during a presentation that my husband and two children are also highly sensitive which helps the audience understand the trait. I look forward to giving many more presentations discussing the trait of sensitivity.

—KARIN OTT

Although many HSPs are natural teachers due to their empathy, love of helping others, and desire to make the world a better place, teaching can be an exhausting job. Karin discovered that even though she was a very competent teacher who helped her students through her empathy, conscientiousness, and intuition, the daily overstimulation dealing with a room full of students was too draining for her nervous system. So she used her skills as an excellent speaker to create a job that is more copacetic to her needs as a highly sensitive person.

Likewise, if you find your current job too exhausting or overstimulating, it's important to explore other related jobs or careers that would be a better fit for you as an HSP. For example, if you are a teacher, you may first want to explore if there are any teaching jobs that better fit your temperament, such as tutoring or teaching in a smaller, less demanding school.

One note of caution is that it may not be a good idea to abruptly quit your job. First, make a list of your skills and review how they might apply to other vocations. Second, I recommend that you begin volunteering in the area that you would like to work in. Volunteering is an excellent way to obtain experience that could lead to a paid job in the future. Another option is to begin working part-time in a new field. The job may turn into a lucrative full-time position.

Before venturing into a new line of work, perform a labor market survey. Contact at least ten people who work in the field that you want to go into. Ask about current hiring levels, salary, qualifications, as well as the physical and emotional demands of the job. Spend some time observing the new work environment. As an HSP it's important to realistically evaluate if the job is suitable for a sensitive person. Pay close attention to the stimulation level, job pressure, and work hours. Even if it means less pay, it is better to choose work that is less demanding and gives you peace of mind.

Chapter 2

Diet and the HSP

A Healing Diet for My Sensitive Body

One of the most important things HSPs can do to help themselves feel good is to follow a proper diet that is suited to their constitution. After many years of trying different diets, I have found that the Indian system of health called Ayurveda provides the best diet for my sensitive body. After following the Ayurveda diet, my health has improved. The body has certain natural rhythms and going against them puts the body under duress and causes dis-ease in ways that are not always readily apparent.

Below are some Ayurveda recommendations that have helped me lose weight fairly effortlessly, aided my digestion, and increased my energy level:

• I eat a warm, moist, and nourishing breakfast. Most mornings I eat kichari, which is a rice and lentil dish prepared with warming, healing spices. I have never felt so well in the morning since I started eating kichari for breakfast.

- I eat my biggest meal at lunchtime, when the digestive fire is the strongest.

- I always skip ice and cold drinks and instead drink warm water throughout the day.

- I found out that I am insulin-resistant, which if not addressed can lead to diabetes. I mostly follow a gluten-free diet, which can be challenging at times, but this diet makes me feel so much better. On days when I have the rare bagel or pizza, I instantly feel drowsy, my eyes hurt, and my thinking gets foggy. Until I went off gluten, I had no idea how badly I was affected by wheat.

- I watch out for sugar in my diet. Since changing my diet, I realized that when I eat carbohydrates with a high glycemic index (that increases my blood sugar level quickly) or sugar after 7 or 8 p.m., I sleep poorly.

- I try to keep a protein bar or nuts with me at all times. Stimuli is hard enough for HSPs to deal with, but it's definitely more difficult for me when I'm hungry or have low blood sugar.

- Several holistic practitioners have told me that my system is too acidic. Filtered water may turn the water acidic. I thought this wasn't true until I had an eye-opening incident. I had moved into a new apartment that had a filtered water outlet on the fridge. I had been buying bottled water but had run out that day so I drank the filtered water. I drank 4 glasses of water but my thirst just could not be satiated and I noticed a burning sensation in my mouth and throughout my body. Now I find that whenever I drink filtered water, I have an insatiable thirst and a burning sensation. That's why I decided to start drinking alkalized water.

There are several ways to alkalize tap water. Santevia makes a counter-top filtration system that I use. They also have a pitcher, which I use in the office, and a travel stick that I put in my water bottle when traveling. As an initial experiment, I ordered a pack of alkalizing pouches from a company called Xooma. The first time I drank alkalized water I couldn't believe how clean and good the water tasted.

—ANONYMOUS

Ayurveda is an ancient healing system from India, based on creating balance for your particular body type using diet, herbs, and lifestyle. HSPs tend to have the Vata constitution, which is the body type that has a sensitive nervous system. By the way, much of my book, The Highly Sensitive Person's Survival Guide *is based on Ayurveda.*

It's important for the Ayurveda Vata body constitution to eat heavy, warm, and moist food. If an HSP eats a cold salad with light sprouts, they will likely become more nervous, anxious, and less grounded. However, if an HSP eats heavy, warm and moist foods like heavy soups, oatmeal, lasagna, and casseroles, the highly sensitive person will feel more grounded and less anxious. It's okay to have more salads in the summer, but especially in the winter try to eat heavy, warm, and moist foods. The Ayurveda Vata body type gets cold easily, so it's best for most HSPs not to drink cold drinks except in a hot climate. Whenever I go to a restaurant I ask for water with no ice.

Some excellent websites to learn more about Ayurveda are Dr. Vasant Lad's Ayurveda Institute: www.ayurveda.com; and Dr. Deepak Chopra's Ayurveda center: www.chopra.com/ our-services/ayurveda.

Two excellent Ayurvedic cookbooks are Ayurveda Cooking for Self-Healing *by Usha and Vasant Lad and* Ayurvedic Cooking for Westerners *by Amadea Morningstar.*

Bon appétit!

Chapter 3

Finding My Identity as an HSP

Discovering Through Twitter That I'm HSP

Throughout my entire life I have struggled with emotional issues. I survived a nervous breakdown when I was 17 years old and consequently endured shock treatment and took twenty drugs daily for a year and a half. I have been married three times and have had numerous jobs. I have had to deal with the death of my parents, and my beloved dog, Molly, as well as an estrangement from my only sibling that is now thankfully resolved.

I have always been a very spiritual person and I remember, as a child, feeling so connected to God and loving everything connected to religion. I was baptized into the Catholic faith and I attended a Catholic primary school. My childhood was a happy one: we lived beside a creek and I spent a lot of my time roaming around the area, climbing the creek banks, looking for wildlife, and trying to see the tadpoles and frogs in the creek. Spending time in nature has always been important to me. Nothing eases my mind or makes me feel more peaceful.

However, I never fit in at school, and attending school was simply torturous for me. I spent recess time hidden under the stairs like a wild, frightened animal. The noise and overstimulation were overwhelming for me. I wanted to be free to experience my connection with God, rather than being stuck with people I did not understand or feel comfortable being around.

Fast forward to my first marriage when I was 19 years old. I mistakenly thought a relationship was the way to find myself. Needless to say, this was far from the case. I was now lonely within a relationship, as opposed to feeling lonely by myself. I threw myself into my quest for answers by reading every book I could find that might shed some light on my identity. Some of the books that really helped me were *Living in the Light* by Shakti Gawain, *You Can Heal Your Life* by Louise Hay and *Transformed by the Light* by Dr. Melvin Morse.

During this time I also became very interested in metaphysics and spirituality. I was desperate for answers as to why I felt so different from others, why I felt like an alien. I began listening to my intuition, and by following my intuition I began to feel that I was on the right path to heal myself.

I avoided socializing with people because I was bothered by noise, lights, and having to converse with people I did not know. At that time, my contemporaries were drinking, taking drugs, partying, or sleeping around. I was so very different and felt out of my element around those so-called normal people.

I kept asking myself what was wrong with me. Why didn't I enjoy those activities like everyone else?

Unfortunately, after another two failed marriages and having a child, I was no closer to discovering my true identity as a sensitive person. However, I finally discovered and joined a Spiritualist church, which was the closest I ever felt to "coming home." However, since my husband was very critical of the church, I stopped attending. I worked in various customer service jobs, where good people skills were of prime importance. Since I understood my colleagues' needs, I was able to support many of them. Unfortunately, I didn't feel the support was reciprocated.

Things took a turn for the worse when my mum, who was my best friend, passed away in 2000. Throughout my life, my mum had always been there for me. Although I was devastated after her passing, I persevered, since my nine-year-old son and my elderly father relied on me. I missed my mum so much but I survived through my faith in God.

My faith in God has been my salvation throughout my life. I prayed often and always thought about God. I used to enjoy sitting in silence in an empty Catholic church and feeling God's presence all around me. Members of my Spiritualist church did a reading after my mum passed, and the information I received about my mum's life was very accurate and I was able to feel her presence.

When I developed fibromyalgia, I had to give up my job and ended up staying at home for many years. My ex-husband was a very demanding, moody, and difficult man, and since my son is also an HSP, coping with him was not easy for us. When my son was about twelve, I asked him if I should ask his dad to leave and he replied, "Not yet." When his 18th birthday arrived, he came to me and said, "If you want to divorce Dad, go ahead." So I asked his father to leave. He was gone within two weeks.

Since I was in good shape financially, I had the time to begin reading many books again, to try once more to discover who I was. One day, approximately three years ago, I decided to join Twitter, since I was so lonely and still felt alienated from people. I was happy to discover that I could communicate love and support via my tweets. This was a wonderful discovery that helped me to communicate from my heart with people. One day, a person on Twitter told me that I was a highly sensitive person. I was ecstatic to discover that there was a name for my trait and that there wasn't anything wrong with me.

I continue to read as many books as I can get my hands on, to learn how to use my HSP gifts properly to help others. Although I still easily absorb other people's energy, I now know how to find a place of stillness and peace within me. By allowing whatever happens to happen without fighting against it, I find I do not take on so much negative energy. I also focus on that stillness within, where I am at peace and filled with divine love. Nothing can touch my peace when I am in this place. I just need to think of God and I am supported and feel so loved. I also believe our thoughts create our circumstances, so I try to think positively and lovingly at all times. Of course, it's not always easy to do.

My life has become a blessing, and I try to pass on my new-found joy to as many people as possible. Since learning about my HSP trait, I am no longer afraid of people, and am happy to meet new people since I put them at ease. I now have the confidence to approach people, because I understand my energy level. Earlier, I would become confused, not understanding why I felt suddenly overwhelmed, but now I can accept myself since I understand the shifts in my energy. It's such a joy to spread love, kindness, and joy to all I meet, which is such a contrast from my life before I knew about my trait. I have changed my diet, and no longer need to take my fibromyalgia meds. I spend a lot of time in my garden, which is a haven for me.

I wish that I had known about my HSP trait earlier; it would have made my life far easier. I also wish that I could tell other sensitive people who are not familiar with the trait that they are perfectly normal. I am now so grateful for all that has happened in my life and I truly believe that I am just starting my real life. If I were asked to offer some words of advice, they would be: "Have faith in who you are and then all things will be possible. Strive to give to others without any thought of reward or repayment. Give of yourself, open your heart, and let God shine through you to everyone you meet."

On Twitter I regularly send love, light, peace, and blessings to all, from my home in Melbourne, Australia to the entire world. It is wonderful to be an HSP. I would not want to be any other way. I am blessed, and so grateful to know who I am at long last.

—ADELE ROBINSON

Adele's story shows us that no matter how much we may have suffered, once we understand our true identity, and have faith in ourselves and in a Higher Power, we can overcome any challenging circumstances. Once she began to understand and accept her natural inborn trait, Adele was able to turn her life around. She was finally able to use her innate traits of love and compassion to help others. When we are feeling emotionally upset, the best way to uplift ourselves is by helping other people.

Through her determination to find out who she really was, Adele enthusiastically began reading many books, which contributed to her process of self-discovery. This story also illustrates the power of the Internet for obtaining emotional support and information about the trait of high sensitivity. Listed below are a few sites where you can get support for yourself or your highly sensitive child online:

- *HSP chat group*
  groups.yahoo.com/neo/groups/hspbook/info

- *Chat group for parents of highly sensitive children*
  groups.yahoo.com/neo/groups/hscbook/info

- *HSP discussion group: Tribe also publishes a magazine for HSPs*
  tribe.paramimedia.com/community

- *Facebook HSP group with over 6,000 members*
  facebook.com/groups/2232091680

The Joy of Learning I'm an HSP

My world changed the day I found out I was a highly sensitive person. That may sound dramatic, but it's true. All my 55 years of not being normal dissolved in the discovery that I have been normal my entire life. This epiphany changed my life.

My mother was quite narcissistic, always craving attention in a gregarious manner, which was the opposite of who I was. She constantly told me that my quiet, sensitive ways were not normal. She unintentionally made me feel like less of a person for being introverted, which was devastating and made me feel like I was never good enough.

Therefore, I spent my life trying to be someone I wasn't. Although seeing several psychiatrists over the years helped somewhat, I still felt like there was something wrong with me. My family doctor recommended that I try seeing a licensed therapist instead of a psychiatrist. After doing extensive research on the Internet, I finally chose someone who resonated strongly with me since she seemed so kind and sensitive.

Prior to our first meeting I filled out a questionnaire, and during our first session my new therapist told me, "I think you might be an HSP, which is a highly sensitive person." She presented the trait in a positive light. When I returned home I went to Elaine Aron's website and checked off every box except for two on the HSP questionnaire. Realizing I was normal, I literally felt my entire being change as I broke down into a relieved, happy cry.

All the things I had been doing intuitively my entire life now made sense to me. I now understood why I needed more downtime than others, why I would find a seat next to the wall in a restaurant, shop during quieter times, and retreat to a bath-room for a break during a party. I discovered that not only was I an HSP, I was also introverted. This new knowledge gave me permission to say no to engaging in stressful activities, which has subsequently improved my health.

My husband was a politician here in Canada, so I frequently had to socialize in large crowds. Ironically, during those years I was told many times that I was very good in social situations and was the perfect political wife. However, due to my low self-esteem, I never believed the accolades, and other people never realized what was really behind my ever-present smile. I was on overload and exhausted, having to attend those political events, and I used to count the minutes until I could wave goodbye and slide into the passenger seat of our car.

When my husband got out of politics last year, I was elated to not have to go to any more political events. I would much rather stay at home with my husband and have a nice dinner, a glass of wine, and watch a video, or go out with close friends to dinner. My husband has been wonderful and more than under-standing through all the tumultuous times, as he got used to my introverted and sensitive ways. We actually discovered, after my husband took the HSP questionnaire, that he is somewhat of an HSP also. I happily discovered that given the choice, my husband would also rather stay home and watch a movie or go out to dinner with close friends than attend a large social event. What a great thing to discover after 32 years of marriage! We are much more alike than either of us knew.

Do I still sometimes do things that I don't really want to do? Yes, of course. For people I love, I will go to a party or event, but I know how to make myself more comfortable in social situations. The best part of learning about the HSP trait is that I know it's all right for me to take care of my sensitive self.

I do wish I had found out about my high sensitivity trait earlier in life. I could have started healing so much sooner. However, I believe that things are supposed to happen when they happen. My wish is for other HSPs to learn and understand how truly valuable we are to society.

I will forever be grateful to my understanding husband, my therapist, Tamara, and Elaine Aron. You have all changed my life.

—TRUDY HOWARD

Trudy's story illustrates the importance of seeing a competent therapist who is familiar with and can recognize the trait of high sensitivity. An excellent method to find a competent therapist is by interviewing three potential licensed therapists and finding out how familiar they are with the HSP trait, and how they work with HSPs. Any therapist that you work with should have read or be willing to read Elaine Aron's books Psychotherapy and the HSP and The Highly Sensitive Person, *as well as my book* The HSP Survival Guide.

You can also pose a question about looking for an HSP counselor in your area on the HSP chat group:

- *health.groups.yahoo.com/group/hspbook*

On Elaine Aron's website there is a list of licensed therapists and counselors who have completed a program with Dr. Aron on psychotherapy with HSPs: hsperson.com.

Trudy's exuberance and deep joy at discovering that she was an HSP is so touching and demonstrates the importance of letting others know about the HSP trait. By sharing information about highly sensitive people with others, you will likely help 20 percent of your relatives, friends, and colleagues.

Chapter 4

Friendship for the HSP

Being True to Myself and My Friends

I never really understood the phrase "be true to yourself" until I learned I was an HSP. I've always known that I had different limits for stimulation than most people. In college, my friends could easily stay out all night, even after the busiest of days. However, I'd be ready to go home after visiting the first bar. Actually, I'd be ready to go home before we even left our house. This made me feel like a loser and I was nicknamed Grandma, frequently told that I "should have been there," and constantly mocked for not being "normal." I'd sometimes ignore my limits in order to fit in, but as soon as it was socially acceptable for me to withdraw from the stimulation, I would leave. Unfortunately, I never really felt that it was all right for me to set limits.

When college ended and there weren't so many voices constantly telling me what I should and shouldn't do to be normal, I realized that I could do things my way. I finally allowed myself to follow my own path: spending a Friday evening reading a book by the lake, listening to relaxing music, or leisurely cooking a delicious dinner. Finally, I felt the freedom to do absolutely nothing if I wanted to, since I only had myself to report to. I learned to accept myself exactly as I am.

As I developed new friendships after college, I began acknowledging my limits to myself and to those I spent time with. Instead of making up excuses, I told new friends the truth—for example, that I didn't really want to go to a dark, crowded, noisy bar. I told my friends that it was nothing personal and asked if we could get coffee instead. I have found that my true friends understand that I'm not rejecting them, but rather I'm just rejecting some of the situations they enjoy.

Of course, there are still challenges. Friends sometimes question me when I say I'm too tired to go out because they don't understand the constant emotional and mental exhaustion I feel during the day. Although I love my job as an elementary school teacher, it can be very tiring. I've realized that there is only so much I can do to accommodate my friends and what they think I "should" be doing. I realize that I should only be doing things that feel right and nurturing for me. After all, if I'm not going to be true to myself, who is?

— ANONYMOUS

Peer pressure for teens and people in their twenties can be very intense. However, as the writer stated, you have to be true to yourself in spite of the pressure to conform. Since 20 percent of the population is HSP, it's possible to find friends who are

HSP, or at least are accepting of your trait. When we try to fit in by going along with non-HSPs, we end up suffering mentally, emotionally, and physically.

By the way, it will likely be easier to meet HSP-friendly people by attending an art or music class, a spiritually oriented group, or a book readers club, than by going to a bar.

Chapter 5

Healing Shame and Addiction for the HSP

Alcoholics Anonymous Helped Me Heal My Shame

I was physically and emotionally abused as a small boy, which felt like growing up in a war zone since I felt things so deeply. My dad would all too frequently use his belt to give me a beating whenever I did anything wrong. I grew up walking on eggshells, not knowing when I would be hit or screamed at by my parents. When I was a teenager I was in a severe auto accident and almost died. The traumatic brain injury left me with poor problem-solving skills. Due to my abusive childhood, I developed the embarrassing problem of bed-wetting, which continued into my adult life.

Since I felt so much shame growing up as a sensitive boy, as a teenager the only way I found to deal with my feelings of worthlessness was to get drunk. I drank constantly, from my teenage years till my late twenties. Finally, when I was 28 years old, after hitting rock bottom, I discovered Alcoholics Anonymous. During AA meetings, I began to share openly about my bed-wetting. At the same time, I also began attending counseling sessions that helped me. Although I felt better, I was still somewhat depressed and intuitively felt that healing my shame would take some time.

I pushed myself to keep attending AA meetings, which had really become a lifesaver for me. However, outside of the meetings I constantly took protective steps so I didn't get hurt. But focusing on my fear increased my fear level, pushing me into a downward spiral, bringing about the very thing I feared, which was the feeling that I am worthless. However, during the AA meetings, I would feel better after sharing about my feelings of worthlessness.

Gradually, over the years, as I kept attending AA and began working with another counselor for many years on childhood issues, I was finally able to feel better about myself and got married. The bed-wetting stopped on my honeymoon, when my wife gave me her utter understanding around this embarrassing issue. Although I would sometimes become depressed by my sporadic unemployment, I kept attending AA meetings and my wife stood beside me, for which I am so grateful.

With the help of AA and my counselor, I made a conscious effort to release the despair that I had been holding on to since childhood. It felt like I was coming home from a war: I was finally able to let go of my feelings of shame. Although I still have my share of physical and emotional issues, I have now been sober for 27 years! I have transformed most of my pain, shame, fear, and anger, into a new, beautiful life. Although I still occasionally feel worthless, I now realize that deep within me there is stillness and peace, which creates a faith within me that gives me hope.

— ANONYMOUS

Although this sensitive man experienced severe physical and emotional trauma during childhood, his strong will to heal himself gave him the power to keep attending AA meetings and seek counseling. Even in the most challenging of circumstances, through our inner resolve to heal, we can gradually make the changes in life that will eventually create inner peace.

By surrounding himself with loving and accepting people, this sensitive man was able to heal most of his early childhood trauma. His accepting, loving wife gave him the support he needed to stop his bed-wetting. The support and acceptance of AA and a competent counselor got him through his most challenging emotional times.

Sometimes when HSPs are hurt, they tend to isolate. This story illustrates how important it is to reach out for support when we are feeling emotionally vulnerable.

Twelve-step programs are not only for alcoholics, but for all types of addictive and compulsive behavior problems such as drugs, codependent behavior, emotions, gamblers, overeating, sex, and work. The major tenets of the marvelous 12-step program include:

- *Admitting that one cannot control one's addiction or compulsion*

- *Recognizing a higher power that can give inner strength*

- *Examining past errors and getting support around current challenges with the help of a sponsor (who is an experienced member)*

- *Making amends for past mistakes*

- *Learning to live a new life with a new code of behavior*

- *Helping others who suffer from the same addictions or compulsions*

If you, a family member, or a friend has an addictive or compulsive behavior, the 12-step program is an excellent place to go for support and healing: 12step.org.

Chapter 6

Healing Through Sound for the HSP

A Sound Program Changed My Life

I discovered the term HSP four years ago. I had always felt like an alien in my body: I felt so disconnected from my body and the world that I would frequently fall down or bump into furniture. I was so spacey that my sister used to joke that it was a miracle I made it to work and back everyday without getting lost.

However, to the outside world I appeared extremely successful, functional, and accomplished. I skipped the last two years of high school and started college at 15, and received my Masters of Science at the age of 21. Even though I began a long and successful career in corporate software, my sensitivity to sound and my tendency to absorb too much negative energy from my non-HSP colleagues led to a high burnout for me in each job. I have held 11 different jobs during my 26-year career.

I would ignore my need for rest and quiet in order to achieve success quickly with each new company I began working for. However, when I ignored my physical and emotional needs, I would start having emotional problems, so that on some days I could not get out of bed. I would ultimately quit the stressful job, take time to heal, rest, and rejuvenate and then start the cycle all over again.

Seven years ago, I reached the end of my rope when I took a new job where my manager was driving me crazy. The stress of having to commute to work downtown in a noisy, crowded train twice a day, listen to cars honking, and work in a freezing, florescent-lit cubicle was taking a heavy toll on me.

I remember getting down on my knees and praying to God to help me deal with my stressful job environment. Very shortly after my desperate prayers, I found out about a special auditory program that absolutely changed my life. The listening fitness program (www.listeningfitness.com) is based on the work of Dr. Alfred Tomatis, a French ear, nose, and throat doctor. The program helps one's brain modulate the ability to tune out certain sounds through the use of sound simulation and changes in frequency. The program also helps one be more present in one's body and feel grounded.

There are two phases to the program. In the first phase, the client listens to music with a headset for an hour each day, with a special machine through which certain frequencies are either gradually removed or amplified. In the second part, the client reads into a microphone while listening to the same cycle of frequencies change. I was amazed at the depth of my emotions that would be stirred up as the frequencies changed daily. At one point during the program, I realized I had become even more sensitive to noise. I could hear buses several blocks away, birds chirping in the distance, even people whispering.

The program is administered by a practitioner who interacts with the client on a regular basis via email or phone, in addition to weekly in-person sessions. As we worked through the increased noise sensitivity, I learned the reasons for the hypersensitivity to noise. Memories of being raised in an unsafe home environment were being triggered by the particular frequency I was listening to that week. As a child I had to be hyper-vigilant at all times because I did not know from where or when danger would strike. So I was always listening for signs of approaching danger. The practitioner helped me resolve this set of memories and triggers.

Once I finished the two-month program, I noticed that some amazing changes had occurred. I was standing at the train station one morning when two trains from opposite directions arrived at the same time and I didn't even notice that they had arrived. Normally, I would have cringed even at the sound of one train arriving. I also noticed that I no longer experienced motion sickness. I used to become sick at the slightest turbulence on a plane or during a bumpy car ride. However, now I can read on the train without getting nauseous. After the completion of the program, I was also able to deal with my manager at work in a positive manner, with the auspicious result that for the first time in my life I have spent the last seven years working at the same job. I also have fewer injuries and am more comfortable in my body and in my relationships with others.

—ANONYMOUS

There are several sound programs that HSPs may want to investigate, to help them tune out ambient noise and learn to go from an intense beta state to a calmer alpha, theta, or delta state. It's important to remember that every HSP is different and what may work for one HSP may not work for another. While the author had a life-transforming experience using her program, not every person will respond in the same way.

For these programs to be effective, you have to be willing to sit and listen to the sounds for around an hour daily, which some people may not have the time or patience for. However, if you feel drawn to trying one of the sound healing programs, please investigate them online. You may have a very healing experience, like the author of this story.

Soothing My Nervous System Through Sound

I was in my forties when I recognized my high sensitivity. Brought up in an alcoholic home, I began isolating early to cope with my light and sound sensitivity in particular. Elementary school was a nightmare, with the fluorescent lights and having to interact with other noisy children. I frequently stayed home from school. But on a positive note, the isolation did fuel a rich inner life for this sensitive little girl.

By the time I was 19, I was drinking every day, and I didn't stop for 20 years. The alcohol helped numb my sensitive body. For an alcoholic, guilt and shame are difficult enough to cope with, but for this HSP they felt lethal. The intensity of being both alcoholic and highly sensitive at times felt like too much to handle.

I finally reached steady sobriety in my forties, through a rehab center program, AA meetings, and the help of a skilled counselor. Using my strong intuition, I felt that in order for my recovery and healing to be complete, I needed to heal the trauma from my childhood. With my counselor, I began to re-parent myself through inner child work.

I then realized that I needed to release the trauma that was ensconced in my body. I began seeing a physical therapist for myofascial release treatment (www.myofascialrelease.com). In this hands-on technique, a practitioner applies gentle, sustained pressure into the myofascial connective tissue restrictions, to release body trauma. This physical release of body constriction also allowed for a psychological release. By healing the trauma in my body first, I was then able to heal the psychological trauma wounds through Peter Levine's Somatic Experiencing Process (www.traumahealing.com).

These energy release experiences led me to learn more deeply about vibration, sound, and frequency healing. As an HSP, I feel frequencies and currents swirling all around me. By using the current of sound through gong baths, chanting, and other sound modalities, I have created a calming environment that bathes me in sustained sound waves. The gong bath is listening deeply to sacred and healing sounds. The easiest method of calming oneself is by chanting, since the body knows how to heal itself. Listening to healing sounds calms my central nervous system and simultaneously soothes my mind, body, and soul.

During this extraordinary time of healing, I learned about the trait of HSP. Consequently, I found a new perspective for my life, which slowly began to make sense. Everyday I continue to learn how to walk my life's path with empowerment, sanity, and health.

I am now refilling my coping toolbox with safer, more soothing alternatives than I used when I was younger. Besides my own daily sound therapy practice, I have incorporated other healing strategies such as hatha yoga, Ayurveda, meditation, high-quality nutrition, hydration, and good sleep.

My work life has become much easier, since I am now self-employed. I have begun offering gong baths and I help people shop and prepare organic, quality earth-based foods and meals. There is a frequency in food, so what we put into our bodies greatly influences our energy fields. I live and take daily walks in a beautiful and peaceful environment in the open forest in Northern Arizona, near the Navajo culture where I sometimes drum in circles. I also visit peace chambers, which are gatherings around the world to heal through sound (www.peace-chamber.com/PeaceChambersAroundTheWorld.html).

The best new coping skill I have learned is that most of the time, in my interactions with others, I no longer come from a place of defensive ego, but from a compassionate and empathic place. I have transitioned from numbing my body to deeply feeling and appreciating my environment as only an HSP can do.

—SHANIN DOCKREY

As with other HSPs who have shared their success stories, the key to Shanin's path of healing has been her openness to different healing modalities. Since every HSP is different, not every healing modality will work for every HSP. However, if one of the modalities that Shanin or others have mentioned resonates with you, you may want to further explore it.

Since HSPs tend to be sensitive to sound, it makes sense to use our sound sensitivity to listen to healing sounds, which can have a profound healing and calming effect on our nervous system.

I'm glad that Shanin mentioned that she found hatha yoga helpful. The purpose of hatha yoga is to prepare the mind and body for meditation, and it can create deep relaxation for the HSP. One note of caution is that some modern yoga classes have students perform postures as a form of intense exercise, rather than the traditional gentle stretching that calms the body, mind, and soul.

Chapter 7

Highly Sensitive Children

Sensitive Children and Positive Screen Time

I have noticed that my sensitive seven-year-old son Jared frequently becomes agitated, angry, and easily upset after spending time in front of a computer or TV screen. Since Jared feels things so deeply, it makes sense that he would be negatively affected by the content and stimulation of computer games and TV shows.

My husband and I decided to come up with a plan, to try to mitigate Jared's agitation. We decided to introduce the iPad to our son this year, but with very carefully selected applications. One app taught him about all the planets in the solar system while another focused on the instruments in a symphony orchestra.

However, the app he has most enjoyed using is the world atlas. He now knows all the continents and most of the countries on each continent. Once during dinner he suddenly started mentioning all the countries ending with "stan" like

Afghanistan and Pakistan. He also creatively builds spaceships from our furniture when using the planets app. My husband and I noticed how deeply he processed and absorbed what he was learning which is typical of the highly sensitive child.

Recently we got Jared algebra and language apps, and he is now ahead of other children in many subjects. His mastering of these apps not only helps him feel more peaceful, but it's helped increase his self-esteem. Other parents have told us what a good influence Jared has been on their children.

Not too long ago we made the mistake of downloading an app that we thought was a gentle children's adventure: we regrettably discovered that the app developed into a game where Jared had to shoot pirates, who would die as they fell into the water, screaming loudly. Jared reacted in an agitated and aggressive manner after he finished playing. We then discussed with him how playing this game would negatively affect him and the importance of using self-control to make choices in life, and avoiding things that are not good for you.

We told him that as his parents we believe our job is to help him have a healthy life. He did argue that it wasn't fair that other children could play violent games and he couldn't. Some parents are not aware of how deeply some children are affected by violent games; and perhaps it's also true that some less sensitive children are not affected as deeply by playing violent video games. But we are teaching our son that you need to use discrimination with technology. We tell him that it wouldn't be good for him to eat only sugary treats for dinner and that, likewise, it's important to feed the brain healthy options.

With the positive apps, we generally let our son spend only thirty minutes daily in front of a screen, and on weekends we allow up to two hours. We always make sure that Jared takes a break every 30 minutes, so he doesn't get overstimulated.

I was pleased to find out from Jared's teacher that our sensitive son is socially very competent and kind, attentive in class, and that he calms down the other children because he truly wants to learn something.

However, if Jared is very tired or upset when he comes home from school, we give him plenty of downtime without stimulation. We tell Jared that he should not just depend on watching a screen, which is outside of himself, but he should also look inside himself to create things. We are trying to help him develop a rich inner life (which is so prevalent in highly sensitive children), so he can process everything he experiences. Therefore, we give him a lot of time to talk to us about what he learns on the apps.

All of these child-rearing techniques for my sensitive son take a lot of energy— so much that I have much less energy for other things in my life. I have learned that it's really important to say no to certain other areas of my life so that my son gets the time he needs with me and my husband; it's important for me to let my friends and relatives understand that I need space and can't socialize frequently. It just doesn't work to put my sensitive child in front of a screen so that I have time for other people. Having to give up time with friends and family members has been a huge challenge, but I know in the long run there is a great payoff, which I can see in my son's improved emotional behavior. I can now say no to nonessential interactions without feeling guilty.

—ANONYMOUS

As the above story so eloquently demonstrated, sensitive children absorb stimuli deeply, so it's important to limit the amount of time that your child is exposed to overstimulating TV shows, movies, and computer games. As the parent in the above story demonstrated, it's crucial to carefully monitor the apps (and other media) that your child uses, so they won't be exposed to overstimulation and violence.

I remember that parents of a five-year-old sensitive boy once told me that when they eliminated television, movies, and computer games, their son became less moody and more cheerful. Reducing or eliminating visual media for your child can sometimes be challenging. However, less time with the electronic babysitter also means more opportunities for positive interactions with your child.

You may want to introduce even your four- or five-year old to the iPad. The following are some websites that offer great apps that can teach your child about geography, language, music, and math: www.touchpress.com; www.borenson.com; www.dragonboxapp.com; and www.worldwildlife.org/pages/ the-world-s-most-amazing-animals-in-one-app.

One highly sensitive man told me this germane story about his experiences as a boy:

"I had a TV in my room that I would watch constantly, since I didn't go out much. I think that watching TV negatively affected my nervous system and probably contributed to my anxiety. I remember that when we used to visit my grandparents' house in the summer, where we weren't allowed to watch television, I always felt more peaceful.

"I also think that watching all the images of tough, macho men had a negative impact on me, making me feel worse about myself. Because I felt like I couldn't measure up to those tough guys and they were all I was seeing on TV, I started to feel like there was something wrong with me. To this day, whenever I watch a violent or emotionally upsetting movie, I wake up with bad dreams. I just can't forget about the show after watching it and sometimes the intensity stays with me for days. Although I would have balked at the time, I now wish my parents would have restricted my television viewing."

Speaking Up for My Daughter

Both my daughter and I have the trait of high sensitivity. Since my daughter was born, I have always noticed her intense reaction to stimuli. However, instead of accepting other people's judgments of her reactions as wrong, I learned how to re-label negative descriptions about my daughter by reading *Raising Your Spirited Child* by Mary Sheedy Kurcinka.

I decided that I would have to stand up for my sensitive daughter when others didn't understand her. Consequently, I was always there to help her when she became upset in preschool. I told strangers not to call her shy when she would hesitate to jump into new social situations, and disputed her former pediatrician, who told me I should ignore her separation anxiety. I learned that I had to become my daughter's advocate as she and I navigated a not-so-friendly non-HSP world.

My knowledge about the trait of high sensitivity makes me feel empowered to speak up for both my daughter and myself. I keep reading, researching, and learning more about the trait of high sensitivity. The phone consultations that I have had with Dr. Zeff were so helpful because he never made me feel like I was wrong. He seemed to understand everything I shared with him about both my daughter and myself and offered excellent suggestions.

I remember before my daughter's second birthday, I was involved in a car accident—several cars bumped into one another while driving slowly through a construction zone. However, my daughter was so traumatized by the accident that she became totally frightened of getting in our car again. My husband, a non-HSP, insisted that I should just put her in the car and drive her around until she felt comfortable again. I intuitively felt that I needed to take a slower approach. I contacted her new pediatrician, who suggested that I give her a couple of weeks before she was a passenger in the car again. He further recommended that I slowly start reintroducing her to the car, letting her see and touch it, and finally letting her play inside. After three to four weeks, she was able to calmly get back in the car and enjoy the ride. Because I used this slow approach of behavior modification, rather than forcing her into the car immediately, she no longer has bad memories of the car accident.

This successful approach has motivated me to trust my inner guidance and not force her to do something if I feel it would end up creating anxiety or trauma for her. I now always listen to my heart and trust my parental instincts. I love my child the way she is, appreciate what she loves, and validate her feelings.

I also spend a lot of time outside in nature with my daughter, since being in nature calms both of us, and gives peace to our souls. We enjoy walking in the park, by the river, and by the ocean. We love to breathe deeply the pure air in the forest and we absorb the positive energy from the trees. A walk in nature is medicine to our sensitive spirits.

I believe HSPs are vulnerable to other people's negative energy. When I spend time with certain people, their energy can completely drain me or change my mood. In my native culture we call people with negative energy *mal de ojo*, which in Spanish can be interpreted as having the evil eye. I do what is called an egg cleansing ritual, which is an ancient form of shamanic healing common in Central and South America by *curanderos* (healers). In my family this healing tradition is usually practiced with newborns and toddlers, who are more vulnerable to *mal de ojo*. The healer runs a raw, unbroken egg over the child's entire body, to release negative energies. After the session, the egg is opened and dropped into a clear glass of water to observe how the egg absorbs the bad energies. The *curanderos* can read the problems when the yolk and egg white are suspended in the water. The egg cleansing is part of our regular routine to help remove negative energies that do not belong to my daughter or myself.

Finally, I want to share a quote that I put up on my bathroom mirror. It gave me strength and lightened my path when I felt overwhelmed when my daughter had problems sleeping through the night: "Babies will wean and someday they will sleep through the night. This high maintenance stage of nighttime parenting will pass. The time in your arms, at your breast, and in your bed is a relatively short while in the life of a baby, yet the memories of your love and availability last forever."

—ANONYMOUS

This story is a great example of how knowledge is power. The writer spent a great deal of time learning everything that she could about the trait of high sensitivity, which gave her the confidence to advocate for her daughter when non-HSPs made her feel like she and her daughter were wrong. The more that we learn about the trait of sensitivity, the easier it will be for us to speak up.

Thank you for sharing your ancient tradition of releasing negative energy. There are many ways to release negative energy that HSPs absorb and it's crucial that HSPs utilize whichever method works for them. One effective method is moving your hands up and down your body and scooping up the negative energy, then throwing off the negativity, visualizing it dissolving into the universe. When you finish the exercise, you can shake your hands to release any accumulated negative energy.

Successful Methods Parenting
My Highly Sensitive Daughter

Since my daughter, Jane, was a few months old, she would get upset when strangers would touch her. Although most adults wouldn't think of touching other adults they had just met, many people don't extend that same courtesy to infants and very young children. I had to teach Jane at two years old, to tell adults, "Please do not touch me." I had to encourage my daughter to repeat this phrase for about six months before Jane learned that she could tell strangers not to touch her.

My four-year old son, Jacob, is not a highly sensitive child like his sister Jane, who's now seven. However, Jacob tends to follow his older sister's lead in certain areas. I'm not sure if he is scared of dogs and doesn't like to be touched because Jane has modeled these behaviors, or if he too is wary of dogs and doesn't like to be touched. However, even if he observes his older sister getting upset with loud noises and with crowds, Jacob shows no discomfort in those areas.

I have found that when Jane becomes very upset, reacting calmly and not escalating the situation is the key to helping her stay calm. Also, talking in a soft, calm voice is a great model for how I want both my children to act. I've also learned that when I give Jane options when she is upset, she calms down. She hates getting her hair combed, since her head seems to be very sensitive to pain. Even now, at the age of seven, she can become very upset when I fix her hair and sometimes she refuses to cooperate. She also gets extremely upset when I have to cut her fingernails since she has a low tolerance for pain, which may be common among sensitive children.

When Jane starts getting upset, I give her specific options. For example, I tell her that we can take a break or we can try another way to comb her hair. However, what I've found works really well is to talk to her about her favorite subjects when I'm combing her hair or cutting her nails. When we are discussing a book that she's reading or her stuffed animal collection, she's not focused on the task at hand and subsequently calms down.

While it helps Jane when I give her options, she tends to feel overwhelmed when she has too many choices, so I limit my choices to two or three. Recently her aunt took her to a bakery and told her that she could pick any treat that she wanted. Jane began feeling overwhelmed with all the possible choices, so to calm her down her aunt picked out the treat. There's a children's song that states, "Stop, think, and choose." Whenever my daughter is having difficulty making a choice, I just sing the song in a gentle voice, "Stop, think, and choose," and Jane calms down and makes a choice.

The most challenging years for me with Jane were when she was three and four years old, since she didn't have the ability to express herself. So I would tell parents of HSCs (highly sensitive children) not to worry, as their child matures, it will be easier for them to express their needs.

I've found that it's very important not to expect my HSC daughter to act like my non-HSC son. Jane can tolerate a maximum of two hours on a playdate with a friend. After two hours, she becomes worn out with all the interaction and then she needs downtime. However, Jacob could spend all day playing with other children. He was able to spend a full day in preschool at the age of three, while Jane never could have tolerated that much interaction with other children.

I was pleasantly surprised that when Jane started public school last year, she did an excellent job of adjusting. I credit the school with being very supportive of her needs as an HSC. As a matter of fact, her teachers both last year and this year, as well as the school counselor, have been very supportive of making special arrangements for Jane.

Jane has a particularly hard time in large groups of other children, so during recess, assembly, or in gym class, she is allowed to take a break and go to what's called the sensory room. The room has dim lights, pillows, and soft chairs. The school counselor, occupational therapist, or a special education teacher accompanies her to the room for about ten to fifteen minutes until she calms down. Another option during assembly is that she can sit in the back of the room, where she feels safe and is away from the noise and commotion of other children.

If Jane needs a break from the stimulation of the other children during class, her teacher allows her to take a ten-minute break and sit in the reading nook area of the classroom, where there are beanbag chairs. However, she's been doing so well in class that she rarely needs to take a break. During gym class, when playing with other children, she feels safer at the periphery, rather than right in the middle of the activity, and the gym teacher accommodates her need.

I know that children who appear different tend to get teased, so I was worried about how Jane would be treated by the other children. Again, I credit the excellent public school that she attends, which has a zero tolerance policy for bullying and teasing. If another child has teased Jane, she will tell me. I have always told Jane that she could come to me with any problems, since frequently children may be ashamed to tell an adult when they've been teased or bullied. I have told the school counselor of any teasing and the counselor addressed the issue directly with the children involved. The children are frequently reminded that everyone has different abilities and needs and that it's important for them to respect and accept all their peers.

I'm so appreciative of all the information that is available for parents of sensitive children and hope what I've shared will help others.

—RENEE ALTERMAN

The suggestions in this story will be so helpful to parents of highly sensitive children since Renee employed some creative parenting techniques. When you employ innovative parenting methods for your sensitive child, the rewards are so satisfying as you watch your sensitive child blossom into a happy, confident young adult.

Renee cogently illustrated how her daughter calms down when she talks to her in a soothing voice and doesn't escalate the situation or overreact. By giving her daughter a few options and discussing topics that she enjoyed, Renee also helped soothe her daughter when she started becoming upset.

Renee became very involved as an advocate for her child's needs at school, creatively working with the staff to develop options that worked for her very sensitive daughter. However, if you aren't as fortunate to have a supportive school staff, or if you find that the school environment is detrimental to your child, please explore other educational options, such as smaller private or charter schools, or homeschooling.

How We Helped Our HSP Son Become More Confident

My husband and I have an eight-year-old highly sensitive son. I (Mom) am Danish, and Dad is Canadian. Our son was born in Denmark and lived there until he was five years old. We now live in Canada.

My husband and I have helped our son become more confident by always validating his feelings and giving him unconditional love and acceptance daily. We always talk with him about how he feels and assure him that his feelings are completely normal. For example, if our son is faced with new situations, such as starting a summer camp, he often feels anxious, nervous, and apprehensive in the days leading up to a new activity. We then discuss his anxiety by exploring what he fears might happen. Sometimes we ask him, "What is the worst thing that could happen?" Then we brainstorm solutions together, to empower him in case those concerns turn out to be true.

My husband and I also bolster his self-esteem by telling him how proud we are of him. When he graduated from kindergarten he was devastated that he could no longer be in his teacher's class, since they had developed a special bond—so he decided to write her a goodbye letter. The letter he composed was truly heart-warming and it moved her to tears when she read it with him. We are so proud of our son for having the courage to share his feelings with people he cares deeply about. We believe that his ability to express his feelings the way he does is a positive characteristic that will continue to help him achieve his goals later in life.

We see his trait of high sensitivity as a very positive attribute, since he has the highest values and deepest sympathy for other people. He recently became a vegetarian at the age of eight because he felt so sad for the animals that get killed (and he doesn't even know what really goes on in the slaughterhouses).

He also cried when he heard the story of Terry Fox, the distance runner who had his right leg amputated in 1977 after he was diagnosed with osteosarcoma, a cancerous condition. In 1980, on an artificial leg, Terry Fox created the Marathon of Hope, a cross-country run across Canada, intended to raise money for cancer research. My son was so upset when he heard that Terry Fox died because he worried about how Terry's mother must miss him. We see our son as one special boy whom we love dearly.

When our son has to enter situations where we know he may be overwhelmed, we take extra time to prepare him for the new environment. For example, a week before school started we went to his new school as a family, played at the playground, and talked about his feelings and fears of starting a new school and meeting new friends. We assured him that he wasn't alone in feeling overwhelmed and anxious and let him know that other kids felt the same way on their first day of school. Since the teachers in our school put up a list of children's and their teacher's names before school starts, our son felt more relaxed and confident having this information beforehand.

During the school year we always work closely with his teachers and inform them about his trait in a careful manner that does not "label" him. For example, we let his teacher know in the beginning of the school year (until he becomes more comfortable in his new surroundings) that he prefers to work and speak in smaller groups. We have also given them a copy of "The Twenty Tips for Teachers" from Elaine Aron's book *The Highly Sensitive Child*, which has been very useful and appreciated by his teachers.

We truly feel that our son is respected in school because of his sensitivity. He is well liked by his teachers, who have awarded him with "Honesty" and "Respect" awards.

Another method that we have utilized to empower our son is that I volunteer on field trips and in gym class. In gym class my son would not participate at the beginning of the school year, because he was overwhelmed by the noise, children running around, and due to his not understanding the rules of the games. He wasn't able to understand the teacher's explanations when he felt so overstimulated.

When I volunteered for the gym class, I played with the other kids, to show my son how much fun and how safe it could be playing the various games. I figured that if he saw me having so much fun, he would join in. The first couple of times I volunteered he would just observe me from the bench, but very quickly he started participating with the other children and me. He finally began enjoying gym so much that I would be the one on the bench watching him have fun playing the games. He became much more confident in gym class because he discovered that he was in fact very athletic and a fast runner.

Since our son participates more actively in class when he knows the topic, we ask the teacher what subjects the students will be working on the following week. By becoming familiar with the topics in advance, he feels more confident and less anxious about completing assignments in a noisy classroom.

For leisure activities outside of school, we have always signed him up for smaller classes. So instead of attending swimming lessons with six kids, he has learned how to swim with just two other children. The smaller classes give him the confidence to succeed, since he feels that he is being "seen" in the smaller groups and is able to concentrate better with less children around him.

— Cecilia Bonnevie

Cecilia and her husband have done a magnificent job raising their sensitive boy to be confident and to learn to love himself exactly as he is. By letting their son become familiar with his new school and learn the following week's lesson in advance, as well as volunteering in gym class, Cecilia and her husband prevented their son from withdrawing from interacting with the other children. By constantly validating the HSC's feelings and giving them unconditional love and approval, parents can really raise the confidence level of their sensitive child. It's also crucial that parents inform the child's teacher of their trait in a positive manner, like Cecilia did.

For more information about raising a sensitive child, please read Elaine Aron's book The Highly Sensitive Child *or my book* The Strong Sensitive Boy.

Dealing with Food Challenges for Our Sensitive Son

Our son, Forrest, has always been a very sensitive boy, and his difficulty with eating a wide range of foods has been one of the most challenging issues we've had to deal with. My son was even fussy with sweets and ate only three types of candy and two types of cookies.

As a first-time parent, I received a lot of advice on to how to handle a picky eater, with most people suggesting that I force him to eat whatever I made for him. I was warned that by allowing him to eat only certain foods, I was creating a picky eater. However, instead of listening to all the advice, I paid close attention to Forrest and listened to my intuition. The more attention I paid to Forest's habits, the more I started to notice patterns in the textures of the food he chose.

I felt pressure to quiet my critics and test my theory, so I decided to offer a bribe to entice my son to eat a certain food. However, Forrest ended up in a crying ball on the floor, so upset because he wanted the treat but he was unable to make himself try the food. In that moment, I knew that if Forrest had been able to eat a variety of foods he would have. I decided that I would have to approach this and all his challenges from a different angle to help his self-esteem stay intact.

My husband and I decided to homeschool Forrest, and this plan worked well with our "world schooling" philosophy. Forrest had been learning Spanish since he was five years old, and we decided when he was ten that it would be great for him to experience a one-month language and cultural immersion in Guatemala. By this time, Forrest had a younger sister, so the four of us set off for an adventure in Guatemala.

We settled into the colonial city of Antigua, Guatemala and took part in the lively Semana Santa festivities. Forrest was overwhelmed by the stimulation and culture shock and he wrote about how homesick he was everyday in his diary. Food was certainly a challenge, but I tried to find some common foods that he could eat. However, what I began to notice was that when he couldn't eat his usual food, he could usually find some bland option, like corn tortillas or chicken. When he would get hungry, he'd go beyond his comfort zone to eat food he generally wouldn't eat.

Traveling to a foreign culture gave Forrest a way to push himself to try new foods. At home, when there was no real chance of starvation, he couldn't find the reason to step out of his comfort zone, so the pushing would have had to come from me: my will for him to comply to make my life easier. One wise parenting instructor told me to ask the question: "Does this action I am going to take strengthen the bond or weaken the bond with my child?" When I would look into my child's eyes at such moments, I knew if I was strengthening the bond or weakening it, so forcing Forrest to eat was never an option.

I am happy to say that Forrest is now nineteen years old and has traveled to China all by himself twice. He attends college and is studying Chinese language and literature and is fluent in Mandarin. Forrest eats many more foods now, but is still greatly challenged by food textures (for example, noodles are still out). My son is still the force behind his successes with food and we remain deeply connected.

—Laurel Rousseau

Traveling to a foreign culture helped Forrest not only to open up to trying new foods, but increased his self-esteem learning to master new ways of living in the world. He was forced to go beyond his comfort zone and used his willpower to try new foods and have new experiences. This successful exposure to living in a foreign country increased his self-confidence so that he was able to travel to China by himself on two occasions as a teenager.

It can be difficult for HSPs to travel to a foreign country since we will be exposed to new situations, and changes to our daily routine can be challenging. When you travel to a new place, it's helpful to take something familiar with you, like your favorite pillow, and look for familiarities in your new environment. Whenever I travel to a new location, I always use the

Internet to find maps to learn how to navigate new areas or contact the hotel where I'll be staying to obtain more information, such as the location of nearby grocery stores, restaurants, etc. Therefore, with some careful planning and preparation, we can feel safe in our new environment and learn to feel more confident that we can handle a wide variety of situations.

Chapter 8

Hospitals, Doctors, and HSPs

HSP Preparing for Major Surgery

My husband was scheduled for major heart surgery that would involve a week's stay in a hospital and a subsequent six months to two years of recovery. Since we are both HSPs, we decided to read as much as we could about preparing for the surgery and what to expect afterward. Our most valuable resource was Maggie Lichtenberg's *The Open Heart Companion*, which is written with the kind of warmth and attention to details that is helpful to HSPs. Because we knew that the recovery period would be a challenging time for both of us, we arranged a pre-surgery getaway to a wonderful B&B where we could both relax and eat delicious and healthy meals before the big event and the extraordinary demands we'd both face.

However, the most helpful preparation we did was giving ourselves a walk-through of what to expect on the day we were scheduled to check into the hospital. The hospital had given us the room number in the hospital where we were to register and which ward my husband would be on before and after the surgery. I had booked a room at an old nurse's residence across the street from the hospital, where rooms were rented out at affordable rates for family members of patients wanting to stay close to their relatives.

About a month before the day we were due to arrive at the hospital, we pretended it was the actual day. I even carried an overnight bag with me when we left home at the exact time we'd need to leave to make our appointment, leaving lots of extra time for getting lost. We took the exact route, found the entrance to the hospital that would take us to the room where we were to register, and visited the wards and the place where I would be staying.

The beauty of the walk-through was that we didn't feel any time pressure (although we did track our time), which is so vital for an HSP. Even though we got lost trying to find the right entrance to the hospital on our trial run, we felt totally comfortable, because that proved that our idea of the walk-through was just what we needed to orient ourselves ahead of time. We asked volunteers for directions, and then we went back out to the street and re-entered using the correct entrance. We took notes to help us to remember on the actual day.

Becoming familiar with the entire process in advance gave us such comfort. We learned where the food court was, how to get to my room, which elevators to take to the wards, etc. We met volunteers and staff members who asked us if we needed help; their friendly and kind behavior made us feel comfortable. We also picked up a hospital guide and map so that we could become even more familiar with the large facility.

The walk-through removed a lot of uncertainty and fears about the upcoming surgery. We then felt secure and relaxed about the travel time, the route, the staff, and all the support provided at the hospital. On the actual check-in day, everything went like clockwork, and we didn't have to worry about the check-in process or how to navigate the huge structure. The familiarity and confidence we felt from doing the walk-through gave us peace of mind in preparation for such a major and stressful event.

By the way, we also listened to meditation tapes specific to preparing for surgery, which also helped.

—TAMARA HARBAR

As Tamara so clearly showed us in her story, HSPs feel more relaxed when they are familiar with a new situation or environment. Also, doing a trial run to the hospital was a great idea, to reduce time pressure and stress on the actual day Tamara's husband would be admitted to the hospital. Whenever you have an important appointment at a new location, it's a good idea to do a trial run, allow extra time, and/or thoroughly investigate your directions (since even a GPS isn't infallible).

Chapter 9

Living with a Non-HSP

Successful Home Life for a Non-HSP/HSP Couple

Last October, my partner of 23 years and I had a commitment ceremony. The two of us exchanged rings and words of loyalty and love in front of about 80 family members and friends who witnessed the special ceremony. After the event, I moved in with her.

Fortunately, my partner owns a house with an apartment on the second floor, so we each had the opportunity to have a separate living space. Since I was used to and loved living alone, the extra space in my partner's house made the new living arrangement work.

I decorated the upstairs apartment in all of my favorite colors, such as yellow, orange, and green, as opposed to the purple, white, and blue colors downstairs. I enjoy having everything in its proper place: it helps me feel more comfortable. Since my partner doesn't mind clutter in the house, the upstairs apartment was a godsend for me.

I am able to relax in absolute quiet upstairs at night, which has given me the chance to process and recover from all of the demands of the day. I'm able to retreat from having to listen to the sounds of movies and computer games downstairs. When I wake up in my own room, I am shielded and protected from the harsh sunlight since I installed dark shades. However, when I sleep in my partner's room, the glare from her bedside window in the morning jars me awake.

Our separate living spaces have also helped lessen any potential emotional conflicts, since our personalities are so different. For example, my phone message states "I am unavailable now," while my partner's recording says "I'll call you back as soon as I'm able." She solves problems with logic and practicality, while I sense intuitively how to deal with issues.

Our choices for sharing a home may be unique, but it works well for us since we have such totally different needs. We have created a delicate give and take that keeps us in balance. When the equilibrium is disrupted when one of our needs is not met, we're both miserable. As we approach our 24th year together, we rejoice in our past triumphs and hope for our continued successes in our future together.

—ELIZABETH CASPER-ROLFS

The key for creating a good relationship between people of different temperaments is compromise. Both partners have to respect the other's level of stimulation, as well as employ creative solutions as Elizabeth and her partner have done.

As this story shows, two people of very different temperaments can live successfully together under the same roof when creative solutions are employed so that each person gets their needs met. It's so crucial that each partner accept the other person's needs through compromise, rather than judging the partner as wrong for having different needs.

Chapter 10

Making Decisions
for the HSP

How I Learned to Make Decisions for Myself

I recognized I had a problem making decisions after I got married and my young husband strongly encouraged me to make any decision, even if it was the wrong one. But I simply couldn't do it. At the time, I thought that perhaps my inability to make decisions was due to my sensitive, cautious nature and fear of doing the wrong thing.

As I evolved emotionally and spiritually, I finally learned that to make decisions I had to go within and ask my inner self what the right thing for me to do was. This process has worked for me, although sometimes it annoys my husband, since to tune into my Higher Self I need to make decisions when the energy is strong. For example, I need to make decisions about long-distance travel quite close to the time of departure, making airline seats more expensive than if we had booked months in advance.

Recently we had the opportunity to buy a small property next to our summer cottage. However, I never liked the property and if my husband hadn't wanted to buy it, I would not have considered it. I remember that as we were inspecting it, I felt an extremely strong urge to back out of the sale. But I remembered my husband's deep desire to purchase it, so I agreed to go ahead and make the purchase. After we made the purchase, I grieved for the loss of my personal space in our own little cottage, which was now going to be made bigger by having the next-door cottage attached to it. I didn't want to change a thing about our own little place since it was my personal haven.

In retrospect, I think fear of change was preventing me from agreeing with my husband to make the purchase, rather than my inner self. I realize that I sometimes needed to push myself out of my comfort zone and experience life with all its myriad of changes. Perhaps the change could bring positive new experiences into my life. The further along we went with the construction, the more I began to think that all these changes might be for my highest good and took comfort in the knowledge that they made my husband happy.

I have learned the difference between when I should follow my inner guidance in making decisions and when my decisions are really resistance based on fear. Although at first I resisted purchasing the new property, I now feel I have the strength and power to embrace this change as well as future changes in my life. Even if I make wrong decisions, my intuition shows me how to rectify and improve upon the choices I have made. I have had a lot of help from listening to my inner voice and I feel so blessed to be able to do so. I like who I am more and more each day as I accept my innate trait of sensitivity.

—ANONYMOUS

This writer learned how to listen deeply to her inner voice so that she was able to finally make decisions in her life. She also learned how to distinguish between her inner voice and fear when making decisions. Finally, she learned that even when she made a so-called wrong decision or was in a fearful place, she could always tune into her Higher Self to find the strength to deal with whatever situations she faced in life.

Here's a great affirmation to repeat whenever you are making decisions: "By tuning into divine guidance and my inner self, I know that I can successfully handle any situation that comes my way."

Chapter 11

Meditation and the HSP

How Meditation Has Helped Calm
My Sensitive Nervous System

I'm a 35-year-old HSP man, and a few years ago my girlfriend told me that meditation has helped her feel calmer and happier. I am particularly prone to being easily overly concerned with world problems. I spend a lot of time reading about the dangers of climate change and belong to an organization that helps lessen the rising levels of carbon dioxide in the atmosphere that has warmed the Earth.

I have found that grounding myself through daily meditation helps release my mental pressures and stresses of the day, and lets me go beyond my daily worries. My regular meditation practice has also opened my heart and I now experience divine joy and love more often.

I didn't feel drawn to the particular form of meditation my girlfriend practiced, but I wasn't sure which type of meditation I should try, so I started researching various spiritual practices.

I read about different meditation practices and tried guided meditations on YouTube. After reading about and trying different meditation techniques, I would sit quietly and ask for inner guidance as to which practice would be right for me to pursue.

There was one particular guided meditation that put me into a blissful state, and I knew that was the one for me to follow. I've subsequently been meditating 20 minutes every morning for the last few years. If I have even one day without meditation, I start feeling nervous and off-center. Whenever I feel stressed during the day, I close my eyes for just a few minutes and watch my breath and I instantly start feeling calmer.

—ANONYMOUS

Since we HSPs have a rich inner life, most of us would be drawn to meditation. Research consistently has shown that people who meditate experience significantly less stress than non-meditators. If you have difficulty concentrating when meditating, you may want to listen to a meditation tape. As the writer of this story discovered, there are many guided meditations on YouTube. There are also several relaxing and grounding meditations on my HSP Healing CD, drtedzeff.com/downloads.

Since HSPs are able to feel things deeply, we usually are able to go more quickly and deeply into a blissful meditation than non-HSPs. Many of my HSP clients have told me that they have reduced their stress level by simply closing their eyes and watching their breath for a few minutes throughout the day whenever they are exposed to stress. Rather than identifying with the thoughts that continuously arise, just observe the thoughts and then let them go. Try putting reminders on your daily calendar or into your phone, to remind yourself to take meditation breaks every few hours so that you will learn to go inward when confronted by intense external stimuli.

Chapter 12

My Best Friend Sensitivity

Sensitivity Is My Best Friend

One of my clients, Anna, shared with me an interesting technique she created to help her deal with the challenges she experienced as an HSP. She decided to make friends with her sensitivity instead of condemning her trait. Anna decided she didn't want to replicate what so many people have told her throughout her life: that there was something wrong with her for being highly sensitive.

Anna decided that her sensitivity is her best friend, and she would be loyal, understanding, and would support her best friend during the good times and the bad times. Previously, she had told me that she would blame herself when she couldn't tolerate the intensity of her office job. However, once she befriended her sensitivity, instead of dwelling on what upset her at work, she began to focus on the positive aspects of her new best friend. She began thinking of daily examples of how her sensitivity helped her succeed at work by acting in a responsible, efficient, and creative manner. She would also appreciate her deep enjoyment and the pleasure she found in taking quiet walks in nature and appreciating the beauty surrounding her.

Once Anna befriended her sensitivity, her anxiety and frustration diminished. She started keeping a diary in which she would write about her new best friend, sensitivity, and each night she would ask herself, "How friendly, loving, and supportive was I to my friend sensitivity today?" She also started sending loving letters to her sensitivity, letting her know how much she enjoyed her company. Furthermore, Anna began integrating into her life many of the suggestions from the books that she had been reading on highly sensitive people, which further boosted her positive relationship with her sensitivity. She noticed that after a few months she was much happier and didn't need to take medication to reduce her anxiety.

She finally realized that her stress and anxiety were rooted in a war that she created with her sensitivity by believing the lie that there was something wrong with her. She made a vow that she would always have a great friendship with her sensitivity.

—Anonymous

Anna's method of making friends with her sensitivity reminds me of the work of Rick Hanson, a neuropsychologist and author of Hardwiring Happiness: the New Brain Science of Contentment, Calm, and Confidence. *Dr. Hanson writes that most humans hold on to negativity like Velcro and let positive experiences evaporate like they were sliding off Teflon. In his remarkable book, Dr. Hanson discusses how during the Stone Age our brain became wired to look out for dangers, such as wild animals, and our brain is still programmed to be aware of danger and potential negative experiences. For HSPs who sustained early childhood trauma, focusing on potential dangers may feel especially important.*

Dr. Hanson shows us how to use the mind to change the brain to change the thoughts. In other words, by using the mind to focus on positive experiences, the brain learns to rewire itself to generate more positive thoughts. By deeply focusing on positive experiences that we have throughout the day, we are actually rewiring the brain to stimulate even more positive thoughts. We can choose even simple positive experiences, such as eating a good meal, someone smiling at you, completing a job assignment, watching a beautiful sunset, etc.

Likewise, HSPs can focus on all the positive aspects that their sensitivity has brought them each day. As HSPs we have the ability to feel these positive experiences deeply, and as Anna so successfully discovered, our sensitivity can become our best friend whom we dearly love.

Chapter 13

Noise and the HSP

Turning Down the Volume

I am a middle-aged woman who has been sensitive to noise my entire life. I must have been born with extremely sensitive hearing since noise that doesn't bother others disturbs me. Attending family gatherings where there is loud laughter and raucous speech is very difficult for me. Even when I attend an event where there is loud applause, I feel very uncomfortable.

I always thought something was wrong with me until I found out about the HSP trait, and I discovered that other people are also bothered by loud noises.

When my husband and I left the usual loud family gathering at my brother-in-law's house last Christmas, an idea suddenly popped into my head. I realized that I could wear earplugs instead of having to listen to the constant, loud chattering. I can't believe that I didn't think of this solution earlier.

I think part of the reason that I avoided even thinking about wearing earplugs was because I thought my relatives might think I was being rude, and I was self-conscious that others would judge me. Finally, I was able to understand that the earplugs were a godsend and I had to take care of my needs regardless what others might think of me.

During the next family gathering at my brother-in-law's house a few months later, there were about 18 people in attendance. There was lots of raucous laughter, loud noises, and dogs barking, yet for the first time the cacophony of intense, loud noises didn't bother me at all. Even though the earplugs masked the intensity of the volume, I could still hear everything while wearing my earplugs. No one at the family gathering even realized that I was wearing earplugs, since my hair covered them. When my husband and I arrived home after the event, I showed him the earplugs that I had been wearing. He laughed and said, "I think you have found a solution!" When I told my brother-in-law that I had been wearing earplugs, I was pleasantly surprised that he thought my solution was ingenious and not rude at all.

I hope that my sharing my success will help other noise-sensitive people.

—ANONYMOUS

Frequently, sensitive people don't implement a solution because of fear that others would think negatively about their sensitivity. However, when HSPs begin to take care of their needs and not care about other's opinions, they find out that most people are supportive and understanding.

Coping with Selective Sound Sensitivity Syndrome

Since childhood, I've been sensitive to noise, particularly the sound of people chewing that I'd hear at mealtimes. My noise sensitivity was bearable until I got married 43 years ago. I then became aware that hearing environmental noises also bothered me.

Approximately ten years ago my noise sensitivities became intolerable due to difficulties with a noisy neighbor (which I later resolved by myself). At that time I began seeing a licensed clinical social worker on a weekly basis. I'd seen many other counselors over the years for this issue, but to no avail. During the five-year period with my counselor, we sought a "cure" for my noise sensitivity.

I was thrilled when my counselor discovered my condition had a name and that thousands of people have it. It's called SSSS, which stands for Selective Sound Sensitivity Syndrome. Knowing that thousands of others suffered from this and that it was an actual condition made me feel relieved. For decades I thought I was crazy.

An audiologist I contacted claimed to have a cure for my condition: Solace Sound Generators, which are mini white noise devices inserted into the ear. I got a pair of them, but unfortunately they didn't cure my problem. However, they do help me cope better with noise sensitivity.

There is also a less expensive device, a white noise earplug that emits white noise inside the foam of soft-tipped earplugs; it's called SnoreMasker Pro Deluxe and sold through earplugsstore.com. Bose noise-cancelling headphones and my white noise machine have also been very helpful. Although my ear-plugs that I take with me everywhere are only slightly helpful, they're better than no ear protection at all.

My noise sensitivity encompasses a wide range of sounds, from the ticking of a wristwatch to the roar of machinery. Even hearing wind chimes or a bouncing ball can be upsetting to me. Therefore, I have learned to employ a variety of coping mechanisms. I always have earplugs with me whenever I go out and my husband and I sleep in separate bedrooms since I can't tolerate the sound of his snoring. I sleep with earplugs and a white noise machine, and use a floor fan to drown out noise at home. During meals we eat with the TV on and I wear my white noise device to drown out chewing noises. I always ask for the top floor in motels so I don't have to hear people walk-ing above me.

I only visit places that I can leave if I can't tolerate the noise. I usually avoid places like crowded theaters or enclosed places where I'm very close to people. Although traveling on an air-plane is very difficult, I'm taking a trip back east in September. However, I'll go fully prepared with my white noise machine and other noise abatement devices. I feel like I can go almost anywhere, and quite honestly there are few places where there is no escape. There's always a way out or an excuse for leaving.

Susan, my counselor, is very spiritual and she incorporated a process called Hellinger Family Constellation into our ses-sions, which sparked an interest in spirituality in me. I figured that since nothing else was working, perhaps turning to God and guardian angels would help. I have tried hypnosis, psychics, and angel readings. I began to pray and began focusing on the beauty and peace in nature.

After pursuing a spiritual path, I have learned to accept that I'll always have noise sensitivity. I feel better about myself since I no longer hide my sound sensitivity. This acceptance has helped me feel calm and peaceful—letting go of the struggle. I have accepted that I will live the rest of my life using coping methods to deal with my sound sensitivity. I am no longer ashamed or embarrassed to tell others of my condition. I realize that everyone is burdened by something and this is my fate in life.

One final note is that I will go to any length to ease or eliminate irritating noises. In past years I've called the police on noisy neighbors playing music too loud. I've also talked to my neighbors about their lawn mowers, barking dogs, wind chimes etc. When I explain my noise sensitivity to my neighbors, they've been mostly very cooperative. I feel good about being able to speak up when my neighbors are too noisy, since it takes a lot of courage to ask others to make changes.

I feel blessed that I have the comfort of my anti-noise devices to survive and a loving husband who accepts my condition and has been willing to make changes in his lifestyle to accommodate my noise sensitivity.

—CAROLE STEELE

Selective Sound Sensitivity Syndrome usually refers to being disturbed by soft sounds, such as people chewing or drumming their fingers. Some HSPs may have SSSS, but the syndrome is not part of the trait of highly sensitive people. Another name for people who have a dislike of sound is called misophonia. There is a Facebook page for misophonia: www.facebook.com/ stopthesounds.

There is also a yahoo chat group for people with Selective Sound Sensitivity Syndrome: groups.yahoo.com/neo/groups/ Soundsensitivity/info

There is a lot of help for HSPs with sound sensitivity and Selective Sound Sensitivity Syndrome, and as Carole mentioned there are many devices that HSPs can employ to help ease the irritation of listening to various noises. Through acceptance of your noise sensitivity and being open to trying whatever coping mechanism works, even those HSPs with severe noise sensitivity can live a peaceful life.

It's important when you feel overwhelmed by noise, to be polite when asking people to make changes, and not to blame anyone who is noisy. It's also beneficial to have a prepared statement when asking someone to be quiet. Try to develop a positive relationship with the person before asking him/her to make less noise. After explaining that you have noise sensitivity, tell the person that you want to make sure that they are comfortable and not inconvenienced by your request. For example, tell the individual how much you would appreciate it if they could be quiet at certain times. Then ask the person to let you know if there is anything you could do to help make their life easier. Finally, you may want to apologize for any inconvenience the request may have on the person's life and thank the individual for being so kind and considerate.

Some of the many ways to block out irritating sounds are: wearing earplugs or earbuds as you listen to sounds of your choice on your smart phone, iPod, or white noise machine; listening to a white noise machine (or small travel sound machine) or a fan; wearing the earmuff-style noise protectors that construction workers wear, which are much more effective than earplugs.

There are now apps you can download for your phone with various sounds such as white noise. The noise-cancelling headphones cancel out the engine of an airplane, but are not as effective as the regular earmuff-style noise protectors for tuning out talking or dogs barking. There are also noise-canceling in-ear earbuds, with little microphones that create inverse sound waves.

Befriending Noisy People

I am very noise-sensitive, and recently some friends and I went out for lunch at a new restaurant. When we sat down, I noticed that the waitress was talking very loudly about her marriage problems to other customers who seemed ensconced in their seats for some time. The volume and intensity of the waitress made us feel like we were at a loud, crowded restaurant in Manhattan instead of in a quiet suburb in the Northwest.

Even though the items on the menu looked tempting, I was going to suggest to the others in my dining party that we leave because I didn't want to have to listen to the waitress's graphic descriptions of her marital problems while consuming my meal.

Suddenly, the waitress, whose nametag read Monica, changed the subject and started talking about how she's trying to change her diet, since she has high blood sugar. Since I'm interested in preventing diabetes, I joined the conversation and told Monica that she could control her blood sugar level by eating carbs with a low glycemic index. Within minutes everyone in the restaurant joined in the conversation about diet as Monica brought us the most delectable dishes, and it began to feel like we were eating at a friend's house for lunch.

At the end of the meal Monica even brought us amazing cookies to sample for free! When we left, everyone in my group hugged our new gregarious and affable friend. This experience was such a good reminder that, when possible, it's better to try to join in with loquacious, boisterous people rather than fuming in silence over people who speak in a loud voice.

—ANONYMOUS

For this writer it was beneficial to join in with the conversation at the restaurant rather than immediately leave due to the noise. Instead of instantly seeing a noisy person as the enemy, the diner creatively befriended the loud waitress and ended up having a positive experience.

While this dining experience turned out positive for the writer, it's still important for HSPs to use their discrimination to determine if spending time in a noisy restaurant is conducive to a relaxing experience. Recently I ate out in a restaurant that was so crowded and noisy, I couldn't even hear the people at my table talk. I ended up feeling so irritated with the high noise volume that I didn't even enjoy my meal and couldn't wait to leave. In retrospect, I should have assessed the volume of the restaurant before I decided to eat there and found another quieter place.

Chapter 14

A Non-HSP With an HSP Success Story

The Benefits of a Non-HSP Learning about the Trait of Sensitivity

Soon after opening my psychology practice as a second career, here in Montreal, Canada, I received a phone call from a gentle, blue-haired punk girl whose presenting problem was that since childhood she could not tolerate the sound of other people's chewing or mouth noises. She had been unable to eat at a table with her family and friends for most of her life without becoming extremely upset. Naturally, her problem severely and negatively impacted her social relationships, despite the fact that she was clearly a deeply sensitive and exceedingly empathic young woman. Her presenting problem had not been covered in any of my training as a psychologist, so I performed much research in an attempt to understand and help her with her problem. Fortuitously, I found Dr. Elaine Aron's website and books about highly sensitive people. I later learned that while some HSPs may be disturbed by the sound of people's chewing, which is called Selective (soft) Sound Sensitivity Syndrome, the syndrome is not part of the trait of highly sensitive people since HSPs rarely have this syndrome.

Unfortunately, circumstances drew this young client away from ongoing sessions before I could really help her, but I will be eternally grateful to her for enlightening me about the trait of high sensitivity. After reading Dr. Aron's first book, I began to recognize how her descriptions of HSPs reflected the experience of a multitude of my clients. As I read Dr. Aron's books and publications, I also recognized the trait in some of my own relatives.

Understanding the trait of high sensitivity has had a huge impact on how I approach my clients. First and foremost, this knowledge has alerted me to the fact that approximately 30-50 percent of my clients are highly sensitive in the classic HSP definition. By learning about the trait, I can address my HSP clients in a manner that does not pathologize them, which makes the therapeutic relationship much more comfortable and fruitful for both of us. I also realized that many of my non-HSP clients have been deeply affected by intimate relationships with their HSP parents, siblings, or partners.

I have also had to think about sensitivity as a factor in understanding my gifted, creative, ADD, and Aspergers clients, as well as my clients with somatic symptoms. I have learned from my insightful and articulate HSP clients that every one of us (HSP or non-HSP) behaves like an HSP in the areas where we have been profoundly wounded, by responding with intense emotional and physical reactions. In other words, I have found that understanding sensitivity and sensory processing becomes relevant to almost all my clients.

Finally, by understanding the physical and social manifestations of sensitivity, I have become more aware of my own experiences of feeling "overwhelmed," and consequently I have made more space in my life to honor my needs for downtime and solitude in ways that have been very sustaining.

By understanding the trait of sensitivity, my psychology practice has been profoundly altered and my life changed forever.

Thank you, Dr Aron!

—SUSAN MEINDL

I wish there were more counselors and therapists like Susan Meindl, who spend time learning about the trait of high sensitivity and how to work with HSP clients. This story illustrates the importance for non-HSPs to learn about the trait of high sensitivity, since it will help them understand and better relate to 20 percent of the population, which will likely include some of their family, friends, and coworkers. In addition, many of the methods that HSPs use to calm down their nervous system would be useful for non-HSPs as well.

I recently gave a workshop to interns at a counseling center on how to work with clients who have the trait of high sensitivity. Toward the end of the training, the center's clinical director stated that if the trait is real, HSPs are impaired! This experience illustrates the danger of seeing an uninformed and judgmental mental health professional—this is why I always ask HSPs who are seeking a competent therapist to interview at least three therapists to find out how familiar they are with the trait of high sensitivity and how they work with HSP clients. As I previously mentioned, any potential therapist should have read or be willing to read Psychotherapy and the HSP, The HSP Person, *and* The HSP Survival Guide. *HSPs can also ask for referrals for competent therapists in their city on the yahoo HSP chat group:*

health.groups.yahoo.com/group/hspbook/.

In addition, Elaine Aron lists on her website licensed therapists and counselors who have completed a program with her on psychotherapy and the highly sensitive person: hsperson.com.

Dr. Elaine Aron's book Psychotherapy and the Highly Sensitive Person: Improving Outcomes for That Minority of People Who Are the Majority of Clients *should be standard reading in every counseling program. As I wrote in a testimonial for the book: "This book is a must-read for every therapist since up to 50 percent of therapy clients may have the trait of high sensitivity. The book is a brilliant, scholarly work filled with many fascinating vignettes and examples about how to treat the sensitive client. It will teach the therapist how to recognize and work with a highly sensitive client by employing therapeutic techniques to help the client manage their emotions, develop satisfactory relationships, and create a manageable work environment."*

Chapter 15

Older People and Sensitivity

Never Too Old to Understand the Trait of High Sensitivity

A grandfather named Charles made an appointment with me, a social worker, at the urging of his daughter, with the presenting problem that he wanted to understand his sensitive grandson better. He loved his grandson but noticed that his grandson would hide under his bed whenever he shouted at the boy. As Charles and I discussed the detrimental effects his actions had on his sensitive grandson, he expressed guilt and was so sorry he had treated the sensitive boy in such a harsh manner.

During our next session, Charles told me that he was grateful to learn about the trait of high sensitivity even in his old age (he was in his early seventies). Not only did he understand his grandson better, but also his daughter, the mother of his grandson. In subsequent sessions he told me that he was grateful that his daughter "survived" living for so many years with a father like him who berated her sensitivity. He told me how terrible he felt that when she was growing up, he always used to tell her to stop being so sensitive, toughen up and just get over it, whenever she cried or became upset.

After a few months, Charles reported that he had a better relationship with both his daughter and grandson. However, he did mention that if he had heard about the trait when he was younger, he probably wouldn't have believed that some people have a finely tuned nervous system. He was happy that at his age he was finally open to hearing about and accepting emotions and feelings he had avoided his entire life. During one of our last sessions, with tears welling up in his eyes, Charles admitted that he might also be a highly sensitive person, but as a man he was never allowed to show his feelings. He said that he had to always repress all his emotions, except anger. Charles admitted that instead of expressing any vulnerable emotions, like fear or sadness, he just raged at his family. During our final session he expressed gratitude that he was able to share positive emotions with his family and finally recognize and accept sensitivity, not only with his family but even within himself.

—ANONYMOUS

This moving story illustrates that it's never too late to learn about and accept the trait of sensitivity in ourselves as well as others. I think this grandfather speaks for a lot of older folks who weren't able to accept sensitivity in their children when they were growing up because they were trapped by the rigid, societal mores of that time. Thank goodness society seems to be changing and sensitivity, compassion, and gentleness are becoming more accepted, albeit at a slow pace.

Chapter 16

Releasing Guilt for the HSP

It's Okay to Make a Mistake

My daughter, a teacher in her twenties, asked me to buy her a ticket to a Burning Man event, since she would be at work. I needed to log in at the appointed time and wait for my turn to purchase the ticket. My daughter and I both know that I get overwhelmed in a pressure situation and I tend to agonize over all the mistakes I could make. Therefore, she and I went over every detail thoroughly, i.e. her login, password, credit card info, which address to use, etc.

I felt so good that I was successful in purchasing the ticket. On her break, my daughter called me and I proudly announced that I had successfully bought the ticket. She was thrilled, since she'd heard that a number of her friends had not gotten tickets since they sold out in 45 minutes. However, later in the day my daughter phoned to say she'd received an email confirming her ticket purchase, but it was for only one ticket. With a little tremor in her voice, she asked me why I had only bought one ticket. I felt devastated. What was I thinking? Why didn't I buy two tickets? Of course, she would want to go with someone. I was beside myself with regret, guilt, and grief.

For three days after making the mistake, I felt sick to my stomach with regret. I called myself names and ruminated on why I didn't make a different choice. On the fourth day I still felt terrible that I had let her down, but then I suddenly began putting the mistake in its proper perspective. Nobody had died, and in the scheme of the world, my mistake could hardly be comparable to a nuclear weapon accidentally detonating.

In the meantime, my daughter constantly reassured me that it wasn't my fault. She pointed out that she had said several times "my" ticket. Although she was disappointed, she wasn't angry with me.

On the fifth day after purchasing only one ticket, a new thought arose in my mind. I remembered that there's a power greater than me and that maybe this "mistake" was part of a divine plan of the universe. I thought that there was probably a reason why my daughter was going to the event alone and that it could actually be for her highest good. So now, a few weeks later, while I'm still sorry about the mistake I made, I'm choosing to be curious about where my daughter going alone to the event will take her rather than berating myself. I guess we'll see and time will tell. So, let the adventure begin!

I'm learning that instead of feeling guilty, it's better to just surrender and trust the universe. We are here on the Earth to learn lessons, not to beat ourselves up.

—NANCY SINE

HSPs who have been told they are wrong for being different can easily succumb to feelings of guilt and become their own worst critic. However, in this story, when Nancy decided to let go of guilt and observe life as simply a divine plan of the universe, she created peace of mind. By being open and curious rather than judging ourselves, we are able to live peacefully in the present moment. Nancy tapped into her innate spiritual nature, to transcend her feelings of guilt and create inner peace.

The HSP traits of being conscientious, combined with deeply caring that others don't get hurt has the potential of creating feelings of guilt when we make a mistake. However, by realizing that we are doing the best we can at any given time and that everyone is human and makes mistakes, we don't have to create a catastrophe from a minor snafu.

Chapter 17

Risk-taking and the HSP

Slowly But Surely: Doing It the HSP Way

I'm an HSP who doesn't like to take risks. "Safety first" is my motto. Due to a fear of possibly getting hurt, I haven't felt like I've fit in with others who like daring adventures and taking risks. Since I'm a man living in the United States, where males are supposed to be risk-takers and never admit fear, I always felt like I was abnormal. I remember I felt deeply embarrassed as a boy when the other guys in my neighborhood would jump off some boulders into the river and I was too afraid to try it. After that experience, I avoided any potentially dangerous situations where I might be humiliated, such as rock climbing or river rafting.

Recently I went on a strenuous hike with a group from work after a company picnic. The trail meandered down a steep, muddy path toward a raging river. As an adult who has now become more accepting of my sensitivity, I decided to try the hike in a cautious manner. Some of the old feelings of being embarrassed for being cautious and fearful came up, but at least I didn't avoid the adventure totally. While many of the other people scurried on down the hill, I took my time checking out how safe the slippery rocks would be so I didn't lose my footing. At first, I felt a need to keep up with the others, but then I remembered I have to go slowly or not go at all.

At one point in the hike, before we reached the river, I noticed that on my right was a steep cliff next to a creek below. I became scared of possibly losing my footing and falling down the cliff. I noticed that there was less than a foot between the path and the steep cliff.

I decided to let the others go on ahead while I checked out how safe it would be to continue climbing down this dangerous path. I spent some time deciphering the safest route, either right next to the embankment or an alternative path further away from the cliff. Although the path further from the drop-off looked more dangerous to traverse due to slippery rocks and mud from a recent rainstorm, I figured that if I fell there at least I would only sustain minor injuries, whereas if I slipped on the easier path I feared that I could possibly fall to my death over the ridge.

After several minutes, I very slowly managed to descend the safer path without slipping in the mud or on the slippery rocks. When I got to the river, the others asked why it had taken me so long. I responded that I am not a risk-taker so I have to do things slowly, in a way that works for me. Interestingly, no one put me down for going slowly down the path. This experience bolstered my confidence: I was honest and I was able do things in a way that worked for me regardless what others think.

Before I became familiar with the trait of high sensitivity, I most likely would have avoided going on the hike altogether. However, if I didn't participate I would have reinforced feelings of worthlessness in myself. From now on, I'm only going to do things in a way that works for me.

—JERRY JOHNSTON

It was courageous of Jerry to face his fear and traverse the dangerous path in a cautious manner. Yet it took Jerry just as much courage to speak up and share with his colleagues that he wasn't a risk-taker and needed to navigate the path in a way that worked for him.

A lot of early childhood trauma that HSPs experienced can be easily restimulated as adults when we are faced with a similar situation of not fitting in. The more we learn to love and accept ourselves exactly as we are, the more our self-confidence will grow. We will then be able to do things in a way that works for us without feeling embarrassed that we are not like everyone else. J. Krishnamurti once said, "It is no measure of health to be well-adjusted to a profoundly sick society." Likewise, healthy caution is a positive trait, and if Jerry was on the hike with just other HSPs, he would have felt like he fit in. Therefore, it's important to surround yourself with people who are accepting of your trait and frequently affirm all of the positive qualities of being an HSP.

Chapter 18

Self-Care for the HSP

Healing Myself, Healing the Planet

Since I was a little girl, even though I was born a highly sensitive person, I've had a fierceness that runs through me. I feel that the intensity I experienced early on was fueled by an acute, intuitive awareness that we need a world that works for everyone, and the current systems are broken. Since I didn't have the tools to understand why I was so angry, I had trouble managing my sensitivities about the injustices in the world, so my fiery personality would create problems in my relationships.

I did not always understand where my strong emotions were coming from but later learned that I was experiencing many emotions and energies that were not even my own. I had been absorbing energy from others and from the world. The fire within me was not meant to be dimmed, but rather channeled in such a way that it served my life's purpose, helping myself and others go beyond society's current status quo, which was no longer serving myself and others.

Like other highly sensitive people, I feel things on a deeper level than non-HSPs and absorb the energy and emotions of others in a visceral manner. As an HSP, I am highly intuitive, with a high level of compassion that drives me to want to help others and be of service to the world. The saying, "I feel your pain" is very real to me.

When I'm not aware of my feelings, I feel disconnected from my inner self and don't know how to proceed with my daily life. However, when I allow myself to be in touch with my feelings, I reconnect to my power source within.

Since my body, senses, and perceptions are at such a heightened level compared to the average American, I have had serious imbalances, both physical and emotional. I learned about my imbalances the hard way when I moved to New York City to start a job in publishing. I stepped into a high-stress work environment and ignored my diet by eating out for every meal. Subsequently, I hit rock bottom in every area of my life, which affected my health, relationships, and overall happiness.

It can be challenging for HSPs like me, who are sensitive to the energy around them and the food they consume. Although it's challenging at times being an HSP, I also realize it's a true gift since I am tuned into my body.

I am a spiritual mentor to my clients, who are mostly HSPs. I've observed that my clients tend to eat a healthy diet, watch positive, uplifting forms of entertainment, and value gentle, nourishing relationships. Frequently my clients are guided to and are successful in careers that are an extension of their sensitivity, spreading their love in in a wide variety of vocations, such as healers, teachers, and artists.

HSPs are at the forefront of positive change in society, since they are naturally very aware and care deeply about what is happening on the planet. Many HSPs just haven't awakened to their power because they have experienced overwhelm and eventually shut down.

I have come to realize that HSPs are here for a clear purpose, which is to heal the planet in such areas as air and water pollution, poor quality of food, and the ubiquitous violence in the media. Since many HSPs tend to be highly evolved, I feel that it is important that we share our gifts and knowledge with humanity.

Unfortunately, many highly sensitive people struggle with tumultuous life experiences before awakening to the beautiful truth of their positive innate qualities. Once highly sensitive people learn acceptance and self-love, they will be able to understand and implement their purpose on the planet.

Likewise, for my first 25 years I went through the dark night of the soul, struggling in all areas of my life as I lived with fear and anxiety. I felt powerless and alone until I went through a spiritual transformation. I remember after hitting rock bottom in a romantic relationship, I put a call out to the universe and asked for help. I didn't want to suffer anymore. I knew there must be a better way and I was finally ready to listen. From that moment on, a new world opened up for me and I could see miracles everywhere. Everything I needed in order to awaken to my true self, to release the fear and feeling like a victim, to get to the next level, was given to me, whether it came in the form of a book, a conversation, or a butterfly. The messages were everywhere and I was listening.

As I tuned into my inner self, I began to feel empowered and my daily life turned into beautiful experiences. I began a daily spiritual practice of prayer and meditation, where I allowed the loving voice of my inner guide to come through and direct my day. This daily practice dissolved my core fears and emotional patterns, freeing me of all that was holding me back from my full potential.

My life's mission now is to inspire, uplift, and share my tools and teachings as an HSP so that humanity can move from fear and powerlessness to a place of love, happiness, and empowerment.

—JENNIFER KASS

As Jennifer pointed out, many HSPs tend to be highly evolved spiritual beings. We frequently personify the teachings of the great saints, such as Jesus, Buddha, Saint Francis, Moses, The Dalai Lama, Amma, and Mother Theresa. If there were more HSPs in the world, we would live in a healthier world, with less war, environmental devastation, and terrorism. It is the HSP whose sensitivity helps create restrictions on smoking, pollution, and noise.

Although HSPs may have been told they are "too sensitive," the truth is that the proliferation of insensitive values has created a world on the brink of disaster. Our only hope for saving

*the planet is sensitive people— being role models and leading
the way, to increase compassion and kindness toward all sen-
tient beings on the planet.*

Never Give Up

Growing up as a sensitive boy, I was bullied a lot, both physically and emotionally, at school. The most dangerous area for
me to venture into was the basement locker room before and
after gym class. I was a target for the most vicious bullies as I
tried to avoid getting constantly punched. I also didn't fit in
with my non-sensitive family, who would mock me for crying
easily. Consequently, I felt extremely embarrassed and shamed
for my sensitive behavior and my self-esteem plummeted, leaving me feeling totally worthless. However, deep within me I
must have believed that there had to be a way out of my severe
unhappiness and emotional pain. Although I believed the lies
that there was something deeply wrong with me, I was determined to find out why I was different and to heal myself.

After being humiliated daily at school and at home for my
sensitivity while growing up, I now realize that it was only
through God's grace that the light within me was not extin-
guished. This little light eventually evolved into a strong willpower to heal myself as I began my journey of self-healing.
From the time I graduated from college when I was twenty-
one years old, I constantly read books about self-healing and
spiritual growth, and sought out many therapists to release my
anger, shame, fear, and depression.

Over a thirty-year period I saw a vast array of therapists, in the following modalities: Reichian, Bioenergetics, Gestalt, psychodrama, Freudian, Rogerian, cognitive-behavioral, and group therapy. I also saw many metaphysical counselors, hypnotists, psychics, and past-life counselors. Some of the books that really helped my healing were by Louise Hay, Byron Katie, Wayne Dyer, the Dalai Lama, and Eckhart Tolle.

Each one of the many counselors and therapists I saw and the many spiritual and self-healing books that I read contributed a piece to my eventually feeling happy. I developed a daily meditation practice and learned that real healing comes from inside. Instead of constantly looking to others for validation that I was okay, I began to focus on merging the little light within me with the greater light of the divine. As I learned to accept and appreciate my sensitivity and let go of the painful past, I began to love life in the present moment. I was able to let go of my codependent behavior as I consciously appreciated and sought out more time by myself. I forgave others who humiliated me when I was growing up and realized that they weren't to blame, since they were just trying to make themselves feel better by putting me down.

Since I have learned that others are just projecting their negative emotions on me, I try not to let negative comments from others bother me. For example, instead of automatically becoming reactive when someone judges me and tells me I'm wrong, I now just accept that it is the nature of that person to act in a judgmental manner. Recently I was visiting my brother, who has made sarcastic, teasing comments his entire life, toward both others and myself. Usually I get very upset over his little cutting remarks, but on this visit I kept observing that it's his nature to behave like that and his comments have nothing to do with me. So for the first time in my life, my brother's hostility didn't push my buttons. I became a witness and felt more like I was in the audience of a play watching a villain misbehave.

I would say on a happiness scale of 1 to 100, when I was in my early twenties I was at about a 5 and now, in my mid-fifties, I'm at an 80, which is quite an improvement. I still feel things deeply and occasionally get upset, but usually I feel calm and content with my life. Most important, I accept myself exactly as I am. By trying many methods to heal myself and by never giving up, I have succeeded in overcoming a horrific childhood.

—TERRY HOLMES

This inspiring story is a great example: regardless of the trauma a sensitive person has sustained growing up, with an openness and willingness to pursue various forms of healing, their life will dramatically improve.

I noticed that one of the writers that that Terry mentioned was Louise Hay. In her groundbreaking book You Can Heal Your Life, *Louise Hay wrote that low self-esteem comes from not loving ourselves. However, through repeating affirmations, we can raise our self-esteem and gain the strength to speak up for what we want. Louise Hay suggested that if you look in the mirror daily and repeat many times, "I love and approve of myself exactly as*

I am," your life will totally change for the better. After all, if you really love yourself you won't tolerate negativity in your life.

Caring for Myself Creates Inner Peace

As an HSP working in a helping profession, I have found that it's vital to set boundaries so I don't get burned out. I can't help others if I don't first take care of myself. I take my days off very seriously and need to soothe myself without any interruptions.

My methods of caring for myself are simple and I recognized many of them in the book *The Highly Sensitive Person's Survival Guide*. Although it took me 40 years to realize that I was an HSP, I had already figured out many coping strategies on my own. Below is a list of techniques that have helped me stay grounded as an HSP:

- I get a lot of sleep (eight hours minimum, sometimes more).

- I exercise daily, preferably outside, to calm my nervous system and clear my mind.

- I eat healthy food.

- During my quiet, alone time, I read books, listen to soothing music, and do journal writing.

- When I'm invited to parties or events, I only go if I really have to, or if I really want to, and if I think that I will feel comfortable there. Otherwise, I politely decline.

- I have nothing to prove to anybody and totally accept that I'm an HSP.

- Whenever I need to be alone, I find a quiet place where I can be alone.

- I invest time and energy only in friendships that are good for me, with people who accept me for who I am, and support me in the way that I live.

When others say something that upsets me, I tell myself: "This is not about me. They are angry at something else and are projecting their anger onto me." I try to stay calm and rational, which I am able to do in the moment. It is later, when I have left the situation, that sometimes I become upset and can have trouble sleeping. Then I try to tell myself, "I'm responding so strongly because I'm highly sensitive. It's okay to be upset. But the other person did not mean to hurt me. They don't know that I am a highly sensitive person."

If I'm still upset, I try to give my feelings an outlet by journaling or writing a letter to the person I am upset with. I never actually mail the letter, but expressing myself helps me get it out of my system.

I don't beat myself up any more about being an HSP. I know that I have to live with my sensitivity, so I might as well accept it and focus on all the good that it brings me. I focus on the positive traits of my sensitivity, such as: I'm able to sense what someone else is feeling and I know how to help them; I can feel tension in a group setting and am able to address it; I walk through life very consciously, taking in all the subtle things that other people just miss; since I see life in all its depths, both good and bad, I get to live life to its fullest.

—ANONYMOUS

As the writer pointed out, once you accept your sensitivity, you will be able to take really good care of yourself. Another good point the writer made was that once you realize that others didn't mean to hurt you, it will be easier to release any hurt feelings. Developing a self-care program like the writer described is essential for HSPs to thrive.

Things That Empower Me as an HSP

By most definitions, I am a "minority within a minority." Not only am I a highly sensitive person, as defined by Dr. Elaine Aron, I am also an extrovert and a high sensation seeker. I was blessed to grow up with the gift of unconditional love from a very spiritually strong mother who allowed me to be seen, heard, and validated for the sensitive child that I was.

From this early cocoon of emotional safety, I never really felt different or weak until around the age of ten, when the sensitive "depth of processing" part of me began observing the world "out there" as being an unsafe place. I intuitively knew that my own inner world was safe, true, and real, and the outer world somehow lacked integrity and I needed to be cautious.

I was born and raised in Dallas, Texas, and despite my mother's love, I seemed to have suffered from dysthymia, which is a low-grade depression, beginning when I was about 10 years old. Looking back at my life, I can understand why I was depressed. I felt like a fish out of water in Texas. The conservative, materialistic values in my environment seemed to engulf me as I watched my single parent mother work two jobs to support us. My family did not resemble the 1950s TV family with the white picket fence. Growing up at or near the poverty line created many burdens that I was keenly aware of and tried to solve. My sensitivity manifested in my extreme sadness about the problems of the world and my own family. I often felt the weight of the world on my young shoulders and I always questioned the adult problems that surrounded me. Growing up in poverty taught me a sense of "learned helplessness" which left me feeling like I was in a jar with the lid screwed on tight, with no way out.

My unusual depth of processing ability and sensitive powers of observation told me something was wrong, something that no one else seemed to acknowledge or be aware of. What my mother and I were experiencing, which had no name at the time, was sexism, classism, and racism by association. I finally understood what those words meant, in my first Women's Studies class when I was twenty-three. Tears streamed nonstop down my face as I wrote in my journal, "Oh my God, it wasn't me!" I still have that journal today.

Through understanding those "isms" and through my involvement with the civil rights and women's movement, I have become an empowered HSP and a social justice activist. For more information about the various types of highly sensitive people, their challenges and tasks, please visit this page on my website: www.lifeworkshelp.com/subcultures.pdf.

Although I was raised in Texas, I really started "growing up" in 1973 when a synchronistic and brief romance took me to San Francisco. My "inner HSP" began to flourish and thrive when I moved to San Francisco. Six months after leaving Texas, I remember standing on a hilltop exclaiming, "So this is what happy feels like!" I had never heard the word "diversity" before, much less experienced what living in an environment where diversity of thought, feeling, and action was encouraged. I just knew that something was drastically different and I felt free for the first time in my life. I was resonating and blooming amidst cultural values that spoke directly to my heart. Living in such a diverse environment taught me that there is no one correct way to be, since we are all on a journey to find our true, authentic self. Thus, I began my own "HSP empowerment journey," although I didn't know about the HSP trait at the time.

A divine inner voice was always within me, but it was hidden by shame, depression, and low self-esteem. It wasn't hidden due to my sensitivity, but from not fitting in with materialistic and conservative values. It was my sensitivity that made my inner world strong and that rebelled against the rigid cultural environment I grew up in.

It was in San Francisco that I really started to pay attention to my intuition and allowed it to guide me. I didn't always know what I wanted, but I began to realize what I didn't want. My intuition seemed to know who and what was safe for me to pursue. Although I didn't realize it at the time, I was actually starting to set boundaries for the first time. I allowed my inner voice to lead me to things that I resonated with. For the first time in my life, I started avoiding noisy environments and began living a simple lifestyle, to avoid stress. Since I realized that I loved nature, I spent much of my time in Golden Gate Park, just lying in the grass, reading spiritual books by authors such as Krishnamurti and Ram Dass.

I instinctively started to focus on my needs, rather than approval from others, which, by the way, has become one of the mottos of our HSP Gathering Retreats, cofounded by Elaine Aron and myself in 2001. As an extravert HSP who is a high sensation seeker, I found in San Francisco novel kinds of stimulation that inspired me. My Victorian flat near Golden Gate Park provided me an inner sanctuary where I enjoyed and engaged in emotional processing. My authentic self began to blossom as I was nurtured by music, poetry, books, and soul-searching conversations with a very good friend. I biked through Golden Gate Park in the evenings to watch magnificent sunsets at Ocean Beach.

Years later, I've been fortunate to integrate all the aspects that made me so very happy in San Francisco into my life in Colorado.

Below are ten ways that I've learned how to become an empowered HSP:

1) Living a balanced life by making time for the following needs:

• Social: Being out in the world on my own terms, seeking novel stimulation, which serves my high sensation seeking needs and keeps my extroverted HSP side in balance with my introverted side, which needs downtime to process, reflect on, and nurture my contemplative life.

• Emotional: Honoring my inevitable emotional reactions to disturbing events and learning to "act" vs. "react" when I find it necessary.

• Intellectual: Striving to learn new things, accept change, and incorporate evolved ways of looking at the world.

• Spiritual: Tuning in each day to a sense of peace, love, and comfort, which I often find in nature, prayer, meditation, and in viewing the night sky.

• Relational: I focus on my needs, not the approval of others. I've learned to identify my emotions, ask for what I need, and know that I may not always get what I want. I've learned to self-soothe my emotional wounds and I've worked hard, with and without therapy, to heal from past wounds that interfered with my own happiness.

- Physical: Quality sleep is a definite key to feeling my best. I also try to walk in nature, which clears my mind of clutter and helps me gain a deeper connection with my own unique spiritual guidance system. Living in bucolic Colorado helps nurture this part of me. I try to do some form of exercise at least three times per week for cardio, flexibility, and strength.

2) Defining success on my own terms, based on my personal value system. This has led me to living a simple life, staying out of debt, and living with values similar to those of the voluntary simplicity movement.

3) Being quiet enough to be guided to work that I love. I was always aware of a higher calling, even when taking jobs that I could at least tolerate enough to pay the bills. (I only took temporary jobs that I would self-contract for as a legal secretary and always refused offers for full-time work).

4) Learning to say no to things that don't work in my life, yet accepting necessary losses as an unfortunate result. I have learned to grieve and let go, which is a work in progress.

5) Practicing conflict resolution skills, and not being afraid to engage and stand up for what I believe in. Honoring the

reality of others, especially non-HSPs. As one of my favorite authors, Anne Wilson Schaef, stated, "It is not necessary to deny another's reality in order to affirm my own."

6) Using my sensitive powers of observation to discern what to say yes and no to, and trusting the process that evolves.

7) Accepting that part of my life's journey includes ambiguity and paradox. Focusing on healing during the process of the journey, rather than focusing on the destination itself.

8) Looking for and accepting the help I need along my life's journey to heal my past wounds and nurture myself. This includes finding and nurturing the various facets of my "inner child" and relieving her of responsibility by showing up in the world as my adult self.

9) Using my HSP gifts in the world, including raising a family within a non-hierarchal environment, where everyone had a voice and where conflict was seen as a positive force for understanding one another better. This positive environment allowed each family member to individuate and still remain a part of the whole.

—JACQUELYN STRICKLAND

Thank you, Jacquelyn, for sharing with the HSP community so many practical methods to empower HSPs.

Jacquelyn's experiences growing up in Texas remind me that how sensitivity is perceived in a particular geographic location can dramatically affect an HSP's self-esteem. A study of Canadian and Chinese schoolchildren concluded that sensitive children in Canada were the least liked and respected, while sensitive children in China were the most popular. The sensitive men I interviewed for the book The Strong Sensitive Boy *who were raised in India, Thailand, and Denmark were never or rarely teased for being sensitive, while sensitive men from the United States were frequently teased as children for their sensitivity,*

I highly recommend that HSP's attend one of the HSP retreats that Jacquelyn cofounded with Dr. Elaine Aron in 2001. As of 2015, there have been 28 HSP Gathering Retreats both nationally and internationally, and they have been life-changing for many who attend. Please visit the following site for current information about upcoming HSP gatherings:

www.lifeworkshelp.com/hspgathering.htm.

Jacquelyn Strickland is a Licensed Professional Counselor residing in Fort Collins, Colorado.

Chapter 19

Sleep and the HSP

How I Learned to Sleep Better

I used to sleep very poorly, which always left me feeling exhausted during the day. I would stay up quite late at night, and consequently would wake up late in the morning. I knew that this was a bad habit, but I just couldn't break it. Then I attended a class on healing insomnia at the suggestion of a nurse friend. The instructor told me to try to go to bed just five minutes earlier each night, and in a few months it would be easy for me to go to sleep early, which would help me sleep better. When I told the instructor that I would watch TV or be on the Internet until very late at night, I was told that too much stimuli at night makes it more difficult to fall asleep: the light from the computer actually stimulates the nerve endings in my eyes, keeping me wide awake.

The instructor suggested that I turn off all electronic equipment early in the evening and, sure enough, I found it easier to become sleepy by 10 p.m., while previously I wouldn't get sleepy until 2 or 3 a.m. Of course, since I was now getting up by 6 a.m., I would naturally get sleepy earlier. I tried the suggestions and within a few months I was going to bed by 10 p.m. and waking up more refreshed early in the morning.

Another sleep problem I've had is that I find it difficult to fall asleep when my feet are cold or my back hurts. I found a product called Bed Buddy, hot packs that can be microwaved and provide instant warmth for cold feet or aching necks, backs, and shoulders. I've also made my own hot pack by filling a sock with rice, then sealing and microwaving it for a minute or so to warm it up.

Besides going to bed earlier, not watching TV or being on the Internet late at night, and keeping my feet and back warm, I also found that the following suggestions have worked for me:

- I now read a book every night until I get sleepy and am ready to fall asleep.

- I don't look at the clock after 9 p.m., so I don't get nervous that it's late and I haven't fallen asleep; and if I wake up during the night I don't worry about how much I've slept.

- Sometimes when I'm feeling nervous, I take a warm bath, or if possible soak in a hot tub, which relaxes me in the evening before bed.

- I bought some thick drapes so my room is totally dark. Consequently, the outside street lamp and the sun in the morning don't interfere with my sleep.

—ANONYMOUS

For more information about better sleep for the HSP please visit my healing insomnia page on my website—drtedzeff.com/ tips/insomnia—or read the chapter on healing insomnia in my book The Highly Sensitive Person's Survival Guide.

Chapter 20

Somatic Healing and the HSP

Tuning In to the Body to Reduce Anxiety

As an HSP I found the pressure of going to school for a Ph.D. and taking the state exam to become a licensed psychologist very difficult. Since HSPs like to process information slowly, I took my time going to school. I first received my master's degree, and then took some time off as I married and had a child.

Several years later, I slowly began my doctoral program in psychology. I chose a school that let me create my own schedule so that I could pursue my degree at my own pace.

Since HSPs don't do well under pressure, I found taking my exam to become a licensed clinical psychologist very stressful. At the time I was studying a process called Authentic Movement, which was created by Mary Starks Whitehouse. This is a body-mind process, which combines movement and dance as therapy, whereby the client becomes aware of the sensations in the body. I used aspects of this process so that I would feel more embodied and grounded during the exam.

I focused on the sensations in my feet while I was taking the arduous exam. Whenever I felt anxiety arising during the test, I would simply focus on my feet and it grounded me, taking away the anxiety. By slowing down the mental chatter and focusing on the sensations in the body, I became calm. I successfully passed the exam, and for this I credit using the techniques of authentic movement, whereby I focused on the sensations in my feet.

Another method I use to feel grounded is to lie down while taking slow, deep breaths. I then put a small rock on my chest and have found that the neutral rock resting on my chest connects me with the Earth energy.

—ANONYMOUS

Taking your time while pursuing a degree can be very helpful for HSPs. When I was writing my doctoral dissertation I felt overwhelmed, so I divided the different parts of the dissertation into small sections that I competed over several years. By just focusing on one area for a specific quarter, writing a doctoral dissertation became manageable for me.

There are many types of body-oriented therapies, like Authentic Movement, that are well suited for the highly sensitive person. Some somatic therapies that you may want to look into are: Bioenergetics, Hakomi, Somatic Experiencing, Rosen

Method, or art, music, and dance therapy. Some mind-body techniques for calming the nervous system are: hatha yoga, tai chi, qigong, and walking meditation.

My Body's Wisdom

I am a highly sensitive woman who grew up in a controlling, abusive household. I learned to believe that I couldn't do the simplest of things correctly, by being humiliated for how I stood, spoke, and for my alleged inability to even walk like a normal person. I would sometimes be woken up during the night, dragged out of bed by my hair, and yelled at for not completing a task correctly the day before.

Like many people that grow up in abusive homes, I learned how to numb my body's feelings and sensations as a way to survive the emotional, physical, sexual, and spiritual abuse. When I felt my own true feelings of terror, anger, and sadness, I was told that those feelings were not real or valid. When I cried, I would be shamed and told that I was too sensitive, and then threatened that if I didn't stop crying, I would be given something real to cry about. The result of repressing my feelings was that I developed a deep distrust for my body. As a consequence, I grew to hate my body, believing that it couldn't do even the simplest of tasks correctly.

Growing up in a disparaging, unpredictable environment also taught me to live in a hypervigilant state as a way to protect myself from harm. This meant that I was in a continual state of overarousal. I lived outside of my own body and used my sensitivity to continuously read everyone else's energy. I would vigilantly watch, listen, and feel my environment in order to determine the level of my safety.

To heal from my traumatic childhood abuse, I needed to find safety in my own body and begin to accept and trust my own inner wisdom. Learning to trust myself, my physical sensations, and how I felt took many years of therapy with a very loving, highly sensitive bioenergetic therapist, Martha.

I learned in therapy that the key to moving beyond the shame was for me to listen to, and learn to trust, the wisdom that resided within my body.

My inner journey toward healing began by creating boundaries, so that I could feel safe within my body. Creating boundaries for myself was extremely challenging because I believed that my body was to blame for all of the pain I had endured. Slowly, I learned that when I listened to my body's sensations and wisdom, I didn't need to rely on reading other people's energy in order to keep myself safe. Focusing on my own inner energy and wisdom to guide me, rather than vigilantly observing other people's energy, resulted in a profoundly different way of existing in the world. When I focus on reading another person's energy, I am in a continual state of being overaroused and overwhelmed with the fear of how I could get hurt. On the other hand, when I listen, accept, and respect my inner being, I am guided by the absolute truth of my own physical sensations.

In order to focus on my inner wisdom with more clarity, I started a practice of consciously tuning into my body's sensations when I was in different environments. I began to understand that my body's language is a continuum, from comfort to discomfort, and when the discomfort is big, or when I ignore it, I become overwhelmed.

By tuning into my physical sensations, I learned how to feel calm. For example, when I walked around my house, my body relaxed and felt comfortable. I discovered that the spaciousness of my house often helped me feel safe, and looking at my art projects on my walls brought me into a peaceful state. I would remember how calm and joyful I felt when I painted each work of art. On the contrary, when I was in crowded places, my anxiety would usually increase and I would be quickly overwhelmed. Crowds tend to restimulate fear and hypervigilance, which makes it more difficult for me to hear my inner voice and wisdom.

By tuning into my body's comfortable and uncomfortable sensations, I learned how to take loving care of myself by regulating my body's stimulation levels. Through reading Elaine Aron's books, I now understand how important it is for HSPs to be tuned in to their own individual levels of arousal, and consequently I spend more time being quiet and alone. Spending time in a quiet, peaceful place soothes and calms my body, mind and soul so that I can interact with more freedom when I choose to enter social situations.

With the loving guidance of my longtime therapist, Martha, I learned to treat myself with compassion. My self-love emerged from the hidden depths of my soul so that I was finally able to lovingly see, understand, and value the vulnerable, sensitive child within me. Instead of shaming myself for becoming overwhelmed in crowded environments, I learned to treat myself with compassion when my senses were overloaded. Self-compassion enables me to move away from an overstimulating environment as quickly as possible and helps me to take care of myself by soothing my senses so that I can return for a while to an intense environment that I am enjoying.

By practicing listening to my inner sensations and trusting my body's wisdom, I am able to venture out into the world more often. After thirty years of painting, I finally felt ready to risk sharing my art with others. I began by displaying my pieces online and then slowly, at my own pace, I started showing my art at festivals and art shows.

It's important for me to complete one project before I start working on a new, unfamiliar piece. When I honor my own pace, I provide myself with the time to move through an over-aroused state when I embark on a new project. I can then move into a comfort zone that comes from familiarity and taking care of myself during a new undertaking. Each time I engage in a show, festival, or new and challenging adventure, I intentionally and consciously pay attention to how my body feels throughout the experience, and can calm and soothe any over-arousal I am beginning to feel.

I have developed a list of "internal tools" to soothe myself and I continue to add to my list with each new experience. Sometimes it is essential that I move my body—by walking, for example—in order to let go of excess energy that can build up when I am overaroused. Other times I need to slow my energy down with meditation, by focusing on my breathing or an object of beauty. All my tools require me to channel energy back into my body so that I can listen to her wisdom and then take the appropriate action to calm myself.

By living tuned in to my body, I no longer need to live in fear of what might happen next. The fear has been replaced with a faith in myself, that I can move away from situations that aren't good for me. I now live from the core of my being, where my sensitivity resides. Finally, I can experience life's pleasures with an intensity that continually opens and expands my heart and fills my soul.

— CHERYL BAILEY

With the help of an excellent, sensitive therapist, Cheryl learned how to listen to and feel her body's sensations and trust her inner wisdom. She was able to transform her life: from living in fear by focusing on others, to focusing on her bodily sensations and inner wisdom to modulate her stimulation level and experience life's pleasures. Cheryl is the author of Healing Through Shame To Wake Up the Love.

Chapter 21

Spiritual Healing
and the HSP

How Intuitive Healing Helped Me

As a sensitive person I have remained open to both traditional and alternative forms of healing. I have seen a licensed social worker at a mental health agency and I've had psychic readings. Recently I tried a unique form of intuitive healing from a licensed chiropractor, called depth healing. It has been immensely helpful for me. For the past six months the intuitive healer has helped me to release a lot of negative emotions, which I couldn't do by myself since I had no tools or means to access them. An intuitive healer is an alternative medicine practitioner who uses their self-described intuitive abilities to find the cause for and heal a physical or emotional condition. Some intuitive counselors may also be called clairvoyant or psychic.

Since completing the intuitive healing sessions, I have seen a tremendous change in myself. I used to be a very light sleeper and could rarely get a good night's sleep. Now I can fall asleep and stay asleep throughout the night, waking up refreshed. My friends have remarked how much lighter and happier I seem. I feel more peaceful and more equipped to meet the day-to-day challenges of living in a non-HSP world.

I recently began going on dates, which used to terrify me before I completed the intuitive healing program, because of my fear of rejection. I now have stronger energetic boundaries and am not as easily affected by the energy of others, especially certain members of my family. When someone says something hurtful, instead of reacting I visualize an impenetrable white light surrounding me and protecting me from the negative comment.

HSPs are here to do very important work in the world, but we need support from those who are trained and skilled to work with our particular traits. I hope you find some inspiration from my story and allow yourself to receive similar assistance should you need it.

—Anonymous

Some HSPs may be drawn to seeing intuitive healers. I would like to caution that many energy healers are not licensed, so you need to be very careful whom you choose to make an appointment with. However, if a trusted friend recommends a particular healer, it would give more validity to the healer's integrity and skill level. You may want to read books about intuitive healing to find an intuitive healer that resonates with you. One resource for intuitive healing is the 119-year-old community of psychics and mediums in Florida called Cassadaga (cassadaga.org).

If you are drawn to energy healing you may want to choose a healer who has been trained in an established modality, like Reiki, which has been practiced for many years and which has scientific data proving its efficacy. Many people have been helped by a wide array of psychics, mediums, and hands-on healers. Proceed with caution, as an energy healer could actually exacerbate a problem if they are not really skilled in transmitting energy.

Chapter 22

Speaking Up and the HSP

The Courage to Speak My Truth

I was patiently waiting in line at the grocery store when I noticed that the cashier, a young woman about twenty years old, was in training. A middle-aged, grumpy man behind me was emptying his shopping cart loudly and intensely onto the conveyor belt. He was obviously in a hurry because he was constantly checking his watch.

I greeted the female cashier with a big smile as she scanned my items. She completed ringing up my groceries before I had the opportunity to tell her that I also wanted to withdraw some cash from my Visa card. Being an employee in training, she had never done this transaction, so she asked her colleague in the next aisle over for assistance.

The angry man behind me in line became very upset. Without even turning around I could sense his rage hit my nervous system, which felt like spikes attacking me. He demanded to be waited on immediately, before my transaction was completed.

He was upsetting the cashier and myself with his abrasiveness, but somehow I managed to find the courage within me to speak up. I was motivated to defend the cashier from the injustice of the situation and noticed the cashier seemed too embarrassed to say anything.

First, I calmed myself down by taking some slow, deep breaths. Then I gently turned toward the pushy man, sending him a look of love and acceptance. I told him that I understood he was in a hurry and explained that I was also in a rush. I asked him to please kindly wait his turn and let the cashier learn how to make a Visa withdrawal procedure, which would help customers in the future.

He was completely shocked by the kind manner in which I made the request. He seemed like the type of person who is used to getting his way all the time, by just aggressively pushing his way through life. It seemed as if he finally realized that he was being harmful to another human being. He suddenly calmed down, his face softened, and he became more relaxed and friendly.

The tension in the checkout line also dissipated as the man told me that it was fine for me to go first. In the new, calm environment, the cashier began smiling as she told me how grateful she was that I spoke up and lessened her stress, since the line of customers had become very long. Interestingly, the other customers in line began smiling and chatting with one another, which is unusual, since here in Norway, people tend not to talk to strangers. The loving atmosphere increased as customers cheered on the cashier.

This experience was such a validation for me. I was able to use my sensitivity to make another person understand that aggressive, intimidating behavior would not help him get his desired results. Instead of telling the man he was wrong or bringing myself down to his aggressive level, the exchange that ensued was about understanding, gratitude, and empathy, which created a loving atmosphere.

I'm normally not the kind of person to stand up to angry men, so this felt like a small personal victory for me and will hopefully motivate other HSPs to speak up so that we can use our innate abilities for the greater good.

—LONE HAUGLAND

Lone showed us that the power of love and kindness can disarm even an angry, aggressive person. As an HSP, she felt compassion toward not only the cashier and herself, but toward the contentious man. She was able to not only speak up, but to do so in a manner that calmed the combative man. One note of caution: it's important to use your discrimination about when to speak up. If you feel intuitively that speaking up, even in a gentle manner, is not safe, it's better to leave and find a store manager or someone who can help you de-escalate a volatile situation.

Chapter 23

Travel and the HSP

Creating Peaceful Trips

I'm an HSP who has to travel a lot for business, which can be very challenging, especially staying in hotels and traveling by plane. I have written up some tips that have worked for me when I travel, which I hope will help other highly sensitive people:

- When reserving a room, I always request a room that is non-smoking and quiet. I tell the reservations clerk that I am very sensitive to sounds and would like to request a quiet room away from elevators, vending/ice machines, located at the end of the hall, in the back away from traffic. I call the hotel two days before arrival, which is usually when they make room assignments, and speak to the front desk to check on the request. I also join the hotel rewards program and let the front desk know of my membership, since sometimes members are given preferential treatment.

- I always bring earplugs, a white noise machine, and an eye mask. If it's warm enough outside, I turn on either the fan or air conditioner to drown out loud city noises.

- I always have a shawl in my carry-on luggage or car, even in the summer, as air-conditioning can make planes, restaurants, conference rooms, etc. extremely cold. I also dress in layers so I can be comfortable no matter what the temperature is wherever I travel.

- I carry a small spray bottle and fill it once I'm on the plane. Every half-hour I spray my face, so my skin and nasal passages stay hydrated. I also skip carbonated beverages, which are dehydrating, and stick to drinking lots of water.

- When reserving airplane seats, I check the seating chart to determine where the restrooms are and try to find seats as far away as possible, so as not to be disturbed by people queuing up for them or by odors.

- I keep a stash of healthy snacks with me, in case the flight is delayed, so I have something healthy to eat if I arrive late at my destination.

—ANONYMOUS

By identifying their needs and being proactive, HSPs can have enjoyable trips. Since many HSPs are shy and introverted, it may be difficult to tell others what you need. You also may feel embarrassed making special requests if people have shamed you in the past for trying to meet your needs. However, the more your self-esteem increases and you learn to accept and appreciate your sensitivity, the easier it will be for you to state what you want.

This reminds me of two recent incidents in which I had to speak up to get my needs met while traveling. A few months ago I called the hotel where I was going to stay several times before I made the trip, to make sure that I would have a quiet room. However, after checking in at the hotel I realized that my room was right next to the elevator. I immediately returned to the busy hotel clerk at the huge hotel and stated that I wanted to change my room. I was told that there were no other rooms available. I then replied that I was sure in this huge, twenty-story hotel there must be one room available, and I politely requested to talk to the manager. Of course there were other rooms available and I was finally given a quiet room after talking to the manager.

On another recent trip, I specifically asked for a room in the back of the hotel, yet I was given a room in the front, facing a noisy street. Although I checked in late at night, as soon as I opened the door to the room and realized that the room was facing a busy six-lane highway, I went to the hotel clerk and asked for a room in the back, which I was given after a few minutes.

By the way, if you are disturbed by cold air-conditioning blowing on you in your hotel room, you can put a towel, secured by some small heavy objects, on the vents so that you

can determine how much air should be released. Finally, there is a website called seatguru.com that shows the seating chart for every airline and warns you of seats that may be uncomfortable.
   Happy travels!

Dealing with Noise Sensitivity as a House Guest

Last winter I flew to Florida by myself for a week to get away from the cold in New York. I have a cousin whom I hadn't seen in many years who lives in the Miami area. When I told my cousin Sandy that I was planning on visiting Florida, she invited me to stay with her. As a highly sensitive person, I was wary of staying in a possibly noisy household since I can't stand noise and have problems falling asleep when others are making noise. However, the offer was tempting since she said she would show me around and the idea of staying with relatives in a welcoming home seemed better than staying by myself in a hotel room. Not spending money on an expensive hotel room was also really tempting since I'm on a fixed income.

   I told Sandy that I have a noise sensitivity and wasn't sure if it would work to stay at her house. She said that wouldn't be a problem. I later learned that a non-HSP's perception of what is too loud can be very different from an HSP's viewpoint. She did warn me that her husband has an office right next to the guest bedroom, but I figured that I would be out during the day when he would be working.

Sandy tried to be a wonderful host when I arrived, but she didn't have a clue what downtime for an HSP meant. She took off three days from work to show me around. All I really wanted to do was spend quiet time at the beach. However, she had other ideas about what would constitute a good time for me, which included a hectic schedule of visiting one site after another: state parks, malls, restaurants, concerts, and plays.

Sandy's husband, Michael, was also very accommodating, but he would work with his radio blasting as he shouted into a speakerphone for hours, even sometimes in the evenings when I wanted to rest. I could hear everything through the paper-thin walls. I felt that I couldn't ask him to be quiet in his own home office, so I would either wear my earplugs or listen to calming music wearing my ear buds. Deena, Sandy's daughter, would use the home office next to my bedroom at night till 1 or 2 a.m., which would sometimes wake me up, even when I wore my earplugs. As hospitable as Sandy was, my nerves were getting frazzled from feeling I had to run around to everywhere she wanted to take me. She also tended to talk nonstop and would get very irritated at the other drivers, as we would hurriedly drive to all of her planned destinations.

Finally, I realized that staying at her house, in such a tense and noisy environment, wasn't working for me. I summoned my courage and told Sandy that I appreciated what a wonderful hostess she had been, but that I needed more quiet time than she did. I asked her to please not take offense and said that frequently during the day I need to be in silence, withdraw to my room or go to the beach alone. Although she appeared a little uncomfortable with my requests, she said she understood. I felt so empowered, not having to talk to or listen to Sandy all day long, and I felt calmer being able to go out by myself.

I also asked Sandy if her daughter could please use the computer that she had in her room after 10 p.m., since her noise in the office very late at night woke me up. Deena was fine with the arrangement. While it was difficult at first to ask my hosts to accommodate my needs, I'm so glad that I asked for the changes, because they made my visit enjoyable and I was able to finally sleep well. If my hosts wouldn't have been willing to make changes to meet my needs, I would have looked for another place to stay.

—BARBARA GOLDMAN

Barbara did a good job telling her potential hosts of her need for quiet before her trip. However, she learned that a non-HSP's version of quiet is different from an HSP's perspective of quiet. Remember, you always have choices, and you never have to stay anywhere that doesn't meet your needs.

By the way, if you are traveling internationally and suffer from jet lag, or even on long domestic flights, there is a homeopathic remedy that eliminates jet lag called Jetzone. You can buy the product in most health food stores or directly from the company, www.antijetlag.com

Chapter 24

Unique Challenges
of Highly Sensitive Men

Making Lifestyle Changes for Inner Peace

About three years ago, while I was studying business administration in preparation for a career in the fast-paced business world, my girlfriend introduced me to the concept of the highly sensitive person.

I learned that there were books about HSPs by Elaine Aron and Ted Zeff, but I procrastinated buying them for a long time. It was difficult for me to believe that I was really an HSP. The following year, I started a new job working in marketing with a new start-up company, and subsequently, I moved from the suburbs into the center of Vienna, Austria, where I shared a flat with three students.

After moving to a large, stimulating city and sharing a flat with three others, I knew that I really was a highly sensitive person. My stress level increased, since I couldn't have any peaceful downtime living in a noisy flat with constant loud city noises. Within months, I developed severe sleep problems, which I tried coping with by increasing my caffeine consumption. At this point, I had to admit that I was a highly sensitive man, and I had to learn how to deal with my trait.

When my job came to an abrupt end, I had the time to begin investigating new ways to deal with my sensitivity. I joined a personal development group, and with the support of the other members, I decided to change occupations. I now I have a great new job as a writer and editor, which is ideally suited to my temperament. I decided to move to a quiet suburb and began practicing a regular hatha yoga routine, which calms my nervous system. My parents, who also happen to be HSP, became curious about all the positive changes in my life and thoroughly supported my lifestyle changes.

When I worked in the business world, I always felt as if I couldn't expose my real self as a sensitive man. Nowadays, all my friends are either HSP or non-HSPs who are able to appreciate my trait of high sensitivity. When I decided to begin studying for my master's degree, I chose to study in a special long-distance program, where the students study online and meet with professors only occasionally. I found this approach less stimulating than attending daily classes.

It hasn't always been an easy journey—integrating my trait of sensitivity and changing my life—but the rewards have been fantastic, since I'm so much happier now. Today my sensitivity is no longer just something that I accept, it is something I've learned to love and appreciate.

I want to thank the authors of the books on highly sensitive people. If they hadn't written the books, I might never have learned about my trait and I would probably still be trying to fit in with my non-HSP peers, living in a noisy city and working in a stressful job.

—CHRISTIAN BRANDSTÖTTER

I'm so glad that Christian began making changes in his lifestyle when he discovered that he was a sensitive man. It's good to begin making positive changes in your life as soon as you realize that you are in a stressful job, living situation, or relationship.

Unfortunately, it's frequently very difficult for sensitive men to accept their sensitivity, since from early childhood boys constantly receive messages from family, peers, teachers, and the media that males shouldn't show fear or cry. Many societies show disdain for sensitivity in males, as the aggressive, macho traits of non-HSM (highly sensitive men) are exalted in the media.

Given societal norms, it may come as a surprise that newborn boys are actually more emotionally reactive than girls. One study showed that baby boys cry more than baby girls when they are frustrated, yet by the age of five most boys have learned to suppress all their feelings except anger. It takes the courage of a warrior for a sensitive man to acknowledge his sensitivity and stand up to society's false, rigid beliefs as to how a man should behave. I'm pleased to see so many sensitive men challenging the stereotype of the emotionally repressed, aggressive male, since for a man to be fully functional he must be able to be in touch with and express all his emotions.

There are numerous books that show how boys are taught to act like little men through a toughening-up process that represses their emotions and creates devastating consequences in all areas of their lives: Real Boys *by* William Pollack; Revisioning Men's Lives *by* Terry Kupers, *and* Raising Cain *by* Dan Kindlon and Michael Thompson.

Many sensitive men have told me how healing it was to read my book The Strong Sensitive Boy, *in which I interviewed 30 sensitive men from five different countries about their experiences growing up as sensitive boys. It was helpful for the men reading the book to realize that others experienced similar challenges growing up.*

Christian Brandstötter has created an important website for sensitive men and people who care about them, with many interesting articles, and I highly recommend you visit: www. highlysensitivemen.com.

Sensitivity in the Lion's Den

During the past 25 years, I've had the good fortune to be a participant in a number of men's groups. Some were better than others, but in every case I gained something important and useful from the experience. Among other things, a men's group can provide a great opportunity for a man to explore and express the more sensitive side of his nature, which may be embodied in a number of ways: vulnerability, tenderness, trust, compassion, grief, deep sharing, deep listening, awareness of self and others, perceptiveness, insight, etc.

For a man like me who is also a highly sensitive person (HSP), a men's group can provide a unique opportunity—perhaps his first—to experiment with the possibility that he can be open with his sensitivity with other men in a safe way. Observing other men in a group being not only accepted and supported, but admired and respected for owning and expressing aspects of their sensitivity, can be deeply healing and even life-changing for a highly sensitive man (HSM) who's been hiding a significant part of himself for fear of being seen as unmanly. But there can also be challenges for an HSM, even in a group of men with whom he feels safe, and part of his growth will depend on how he faces those challenges when they occur.

I was once a member of a peer-facilitated men's group. As there was no "authority figure" (counselor or therapist) present, it was up to each of us, as individual group members, to maintain the safety of the group. We began every group meeting by giving each member the opportunity to check in and share whatever was up for him at that time. During one such check-in, I told everyone about an all-day monster headache (I believe I called it a "rhino killer") that had almost convinced me not to come to group that evening. I wasn't fishing for sympathy or praise; I simply wanted everyone to know that I wasn't feeling well, that I wasn't at my best, and that it had been a bit of a struggle to join them that day.

Much to my surprise, one of the other group members responded by telling me to "stop whining and just get on with things." I was stunned and very upset to receive such a power-fully critical reaction in what was supposed to be a safe environment where we could all be open and honest about whatever we had going on. I felt profoundly shamed and invalidated. Shocked, rattled, and unsure of what I should do, I kept my feelings to myself (as HSPs are often prone to do immediately after what feels like a surprise attack) and completed the meeting as best I could.

Our group met bi-weekly, so I had a full two weeks to process my experience and review my options. I thought about leaving the group, as it no longer felt like the safe environment I'd thought it was, but decided to attend one more meeting and talk about what had happened previously as the first order of business. The meeting location for the group rotated from member to member each time, and as it happened the next meeting was being held in the home of the fellow who'd told me to "stop whining."

I felt like I was walking into the lion's den that evening, but I kept my commitment to myself. I spoke honestly about what I'd experienced, defined limits about what I found helpful and unhelpful in terms of feedback, and expressed my expectations for how I was to be treated in the group. The result was a very productive discussion about what had happened during our last meeting, how we all might have handled the situation differently, and what I needed from everyone to continue my participation. Everyone, including the "lion," expressed appreciation to me for my courage in showing up and stating my position and my needs so clearly. And they all said they'd learned something from the way I did it.

My point in sharing this story is that it's important for those of us who are HSPs (male or female) to use the skills we have to assert ourselves and our needs when similar challenging opportunities present themselves to us, as they inevitably will in a world that often feels so hostile and unfriendly to our very nature. We need to do this not only for our own sake, but also for those who may benefit from seeing the strength and clarity that we sensitive folks often hide, even from ourselves. Taking action on our own behalf will not always yield the outcome we desire, but we can only get stronger with practice.

—RICK BELDEN

This eloquently written story by Rick Belden illustrates the need for HSPs to speak up when they are hurt. Since highly sensitive men have been shamed growing up for not meeting society's false criteria of what being a man is, it may be initially challenging for the HSM to stand up to an aggressive person.

I also remember being humiliated by an aggressive male in a men's group that I attended some years ago, and sitting there fuming for the rest of the meeting. Since men have been inculcated with society's values that men should act tough, even in a men's processing group the other men in the group probably also felt intimidated by the alpha bully, so no one spoke up in my defense or acknowledged how uncomfortable I felt.

Like Rick, I thought of quitting the group, but finally decided to return to speak my truth. Although I had some fear of confronting the bully, I felt that some of the other guys in the group would support me and I knew that I had to speak up. Subsequently, my feelings were validated, the alpha male apologized, and my speaking up made a positive lasting impact on the group. The members of the group became more compassionate toward one another and I realized how HSPs are doing a great service to the world by sharing their truth by speaking up. If you need help speaking up, you may want to role-play with a friend or family member.

Attending a men's group is one of the few places where men can express their full range of emotions, explore what it really means to be a man, and express their true feelings in the company of other men. As Rick mentioned, participating in a men's group can be quite a healing experience for men who have been humiliated for being sensitive growing up.

If a sensitive man is interested in joining a men's group, he will want to observe the group during an initial visit to explore if the group feels safe. It would be beneficial to state clearly how he expects to be treated by the other participants in one of the early sessions. To find a men's group in your area, just search the Internet for men's groups and the name of your city.

Rick Belden has written many uplifting articles about the true meaning of masculinity and highly sensitive people. He is the author of Iron Man Family Outing: Poems about Transition into a More Conscious Manhood. Please visit his website: Rickbelden.com

Chapter 25

Working Through Grief for the HSP

Coping with the Death of My Beautiful, Sensitive Son

Even after we brought my son home to die, we were not prepared for the effect it would have on us. In the background were the hushed sounds of Ben's ventilator and the shuffling of visitors' feet as they came to pay their last respects. The tragic scene took place in our living room, which was the place where our family was meant to enjoy good times for the next 20 years. Now Ben's hospital bed commanded center stage and I knew his time on Earth was drawing to a close. As I stared intently into his face, no longer trying to have him sit up, I had to accept that he was too far gone. I simply told him about all the people who had visited him and loved him.

I spoke gently to my son, in the hope that as he died he would feel safe, calm, and loved. I wanted to believe that as he took his last breath, he would be heading to a beautiful, bright light surrounded by an eternity of love. I surrendered to the moment and just kept reassuring my beautiful child that he would be all right. Suddenly, Ben took one enormous gasp and opened his eyes so wide that I jumped in fright. I saw right into the depths of his being. It was a moment I will never forget, burnt into my memory. It was divinely perfect that my husband and I were right there, staring into his face. That enormous gasp was Ben's last breath and I stared into his beautiful eyes before they closed forever.

How can a highly sensitive mother move forward from that devastating experience? I had to move baby step by baby step, minute by minute, hour by hour, and day by day. During the three months of Ben's illness I had surrendered totally, since I thought that I must become ready to face the inevitable. Whenever I needed to cry, I cried. Whenever I felt angry, I let myself be angry. A friend said I ought to have a bumper sticker stating, "Grieving parent, anything goes." I had some beliefs that helped me: "You only get what you can cope with," "This world is too harsh for my exquisitely sensitive son," and "He is better off where he's going."

While my son was dying, I had to believe that something good would come out of this tragedy. Day by day, I just focused on whatever presented itself to me at any given moment. I had to deal with my Ben lying unconscious on the hospital bed while the pressure in his head built, with his neurosurgeon being fairly unresponsive to my pleas, with my daughter having a meltdown at school. My beliefs guided my way to my responses during this tumultuous time and it was a comfort that my beliefs made intuitive sense to me.

As an HSP, I just knew that I had to cope for the sake of my daughter, Sami. My empathy for her was my overriding emotion. If she hadn't been around, it would have been much more difficult to move forward, but Sami deserved the fullest life possible despite our family tragedy. Surprisingly, one week after the funeral the perfect part-time job was presented to me. I had not worked for the past ten years while raising my children, but I just knew, despite my recent tragedy and overwhelming grief, I had to apply. The job involved selling medication for Parkinson's disease and schizophrenia to neurologists and psychiatrists.

I had never met a neurologist until Ben became sick and now a job was available in that field. There really are no coincidences, so I rose to the challenge as I remembered the saying, "Feel the fear and do it anyway." Taking the job was difficult for my daughter as she felt further abandonment, yet I managed to juggle both my daughter's schedule and my new job. I remembered my husband telling me that his parents weren't available to him when his brother died at a similar age, so Sami became my predominant focus. Therefore, I was determined to keep on pushing myself through my intense emotions. I have now been successfully working in the same job for three years.

Probably the most difficult ongoing part of this tragedy involves my daughter, Sami, since she lost not only her brother, but a very close playmate and confidant. Early in my grief, I would focus on finding even the tiniest good that was happening in my life. I refused to focus on "Why me?" and "It's not fair." If Sami smiled, a friend showed her kindness, or she had an opportunity to play with a boy (as sort of a fill-in for Ben), then I could feel that there was some good that day.

I read a wonderful article that stated that life is 90 percent attitude and only 10 percent of what happens to us. I don't think my Ben's dying was only 10 percent, but the point is that I really can choose to focus on what I gained by having him and not what I lost. This attitude requires constant reinforcement and refocusing, but it really can positively affect my mood at any given time.

Perhaps eight months after Ben passed away, I read Elaine Aron's book, *The Highly Sensitive Child* and everything started to make sense. Ben was the most highly sensitive child I had ever met. My parenting involved enormous consideration about how to support him so that he would feel confident and capable in this overwhelming world. He was so thoughtful that it has nearly made sense that he died, so I could raise awareness here in Australia and help other parents support their own sweet highly sensitive children.

Another book that really resonated with me and helped me deal with my grief was Victor Frankl's *Man's Search for Meaning*. Victor Frankl was a holocaust survivor who spent three years in concentration camps and whose parents, pregnant wife, and brother all perished during World War II. He wrote that having a higher purpose in life to aspire to involves helping others, which then increases one's happiness.

Now, three years after Ben's passing, I focus on supporting my daughter to realize her full potential and am starting a consulting business to help highly sensitivity children. I've also been working with a wonderful bioenergy healer, which has also helped me immensely, to heal my emotions. It's also worth noting that sometimes taking medication for depression and anxiety can help HSPs during crises. I have remained open to all methods of healing in order to find inner peace.

I feel compelled to keep pushing forward with my quest to help my daughter and other sensitive children, and I trust that as I leave this Earth, everything will finally make sense. I am writing a book called *Ben's Story: A Highly Sensitive Child*. I am also obtaining a degree in counseling, so I can counsel other parents and children. I would also like to give talks about my experiences as a HSP mom who learned how to cope with such an enormous tragedy.

—SALLY GAGE

Sally's poignant story about how she managed to cope after the death of her little boy is so touching and heartbreaking, yet inspirational. HSPs have the inner strength to keep moving forward, especially when we use our natural empathy to help others, like Sally has done with her daughter and through helping other sensitive children.

Although we may feel tragedy deeper than others, we can use our innate intuition to pull ourselves out of despair by being, like Sally, open to many healing modalities.

Sally coordinates a group for HSPs and parents of highly sensitive children in the Gold Coast, Australia. For more information please visit:

www.highlysensitivekids.com.au.

Thank you, Sally, for sharing your inspiration and love.

Conclusion

Now that you have read so many success stories by highly sensitive people, you will likely be inspired to employ many of the new, positive techniques in your life. The more you focus on your successes in the present, the more past difficulties and challenges will cease to be important. The time has come to accept and embrace all of the positive aspects of your trait of high sensitivity. Remember, there are millions of other HSPs throughout the world who are learning to love and appreciate their sensitivity just like the contributors of these stories.

My wish is that all of the uplifting and practical success stories that HSPs have shared throughout this book will motivate and inspire everyone throughout the HSP world community to live a peaceful and fulfilling life. As we learn to recognize, embrace, and manifest our many gifts as sensitive people, we will not only empower ourselves, but will make the world a healthier, more loving and compassionate place for people, animals, and Mother Nature.

Resources

Information on Selecting
Healing Modalities for the HSP

Since each HSP is unique, a method that helps one HSP could possibly have an adverse effect on another. I recommend that you consult with your doctor before starting any alternative healing program. You need to carefully review each modality and also use your intuition to discover which healing modality is best for you. It would be good to spend some time researching each of the websites and books listed below and note if any of the methods seem to resonate with you. There are many types of healing techniques: I have not provided a comprehensive list of them. If you are interested in a healing technique that has not been presented below, please use the same criteria to investigate whether it is appropriate for you. The list below is compiled from experiences of the HSP contributors to this book and from my own research.

The quality of treatments and practitioners varies, so I can't promise that the one you choose will meet your expectations. As with any healing modality, it is up to you to select carefully and with as much knowledge as possible. I believe the information below will be a good start to your research.

Publication information about the books listed below is located in the following References section.

Career
Books:

The Highly Sensitive Person by Elaine Aron, chapter 6

The HSP Survival Guide by Ted Zeff, chapter 7

Making Work Work for the Highly Sensitive Person by Barrie Jaeger

The Power of Sensitivity, chapter 1

Diet
Books:

Ayurvedic Cooking for Self-Healing by Usha and Vasant Lad

Ayurvedic Cooking for Westerners by Amadea Morningstar

The HSP Survival Guide by Ted Zeff, chapter 4

The Power of Sensitivity, chapter 2

Finding an HSP Counselor/Therapist and Groups
Books:

HSP self- healing and starting an HSP group:

The Highly Sensitive Person's Workbook by Elaine Aron

Recommended reading for your therapist/counselor:

Psychotherapy and the Highly Sensitive Person: Improving Outcomes for That Minority of People Who Are the Majority of Clients by Elaine Aron

Websites:

Connect with other HSPs who may know of an HSP counselor/therapist in your area: health.groups.yahoo.com/group/hspbook

Consultations with Ted Zeff, (phone, Skype, or in person):

drtedzeff.com/appointments

Dr. Elaine Aron's list of licensed therapists and counselors who have completed a program on psychotherapy with HSPs:

www.hsperson.com

HSP Facebook page: facebook.com/groups/2232091680

HSP discussion group: Tribe (also publishes a magazine for HSPs):

tribe.paramimedia.com/community

HSP Gatherings: www.lifeworkshelp.com/hspgathering.htm

HSP meet-up group in your area, which includes a list of 38 groups in 36 cities in seven countries: earon.meetup.com

Finding My Identify as an HSP

Books:

The Highly Sensitive Person by Elaine Aron

Websites:

Detailed information about the trait of HSP: hsperson.com

Self-tests for HSPs: hsperson.com/test

Jacquelyn Strickland's types of HSPs, challenges, and tasks:
www.lifeworkshelp.com/subcultures.pdf

Healing Addiction

Books:

The Power of Sensitivity, chapter 5

Websites:

Twelve-step programs: 12step.org

Healing Through Sound

Books:

The Power of Sensitivity, chapter 6

Websites:

Gong baths (listening to sacred and healing sounds):
earthgongbath.com

Listening fitness sound program: www.listeningfitness.com

Highly Sensitive Children

Books:

The Highly Sensitive Child by Elaine Aron

The Power of Sensitivity, chapter 7

The Strong Sensitive Boy by Ted Zeff

Websites:

Chat group for parents of highly sensitive children: groups.yahoo.com/neo/groups/hscbook/info

Sally Gage's site for HSPs and parents of HSCs in Australia: www.highlysensitivekids.com.au

Highly Sensitive Men

Books:

Iron Man Family Outing: Poems About Transition Into a More Conscious Manhood by Rick Belden

The Power of Sensitivity, chapter 24

Raising Cain by Dan Kindlon and Michael Thompson

Real Boys by William Pollack

The Strong Sensitive Boy by Ted Zeff

Websites:

Christian Brandstötter's website, with many interesting articles about highly sensitive men: www.highlysensitivemen.com

Rick Belden's website, with many uplifting articles about the true meaning of masculinity and highly sensitive people: Rickbelden.com

Living with a Non-HSP

Books:

The Highly Sensitive Person by Elaine Aron, chapter 7

The Highly Sensitive Person in Love by Elaine Aron

The HSP Survival Guide by Ted Zeff, chapter 6

The Power of Sensitivity, chapter 9

Meditation

Books:

The Power of Sensitivity, chapter 11

Websites:

Buddhist meditation: www. buddhanet.net

Integrated Amrita Meditation Technique:

amma.org/groups/north-america/projects/iam-meditation-classes

Mindfulness Meditation: www.plumvillage.org

Self-Realization Fellowship: www.yogananda-srf.org

Ted Zeff's guided meditation/visualization CD: drtedzeff.com/downloads

Transcendental Meditation: www.tm.org

Vipassana Meditation: www.inquiringmind.com

Noise

Books:

The Power of Sensitivity, chapter 13

Websites:

Noise Pollution Clearinghouse, (national nonprofit organization with online noise-related resources): www.nonoise.org

Selective Sound Sensitivity Syndrome Facebook page:

www.facebook.com/stopthesounds

White noise earplug that emits white noise inside the foam of soft-tipped earplugs called SnoreMasker Pro Deluxe: earplugstore.com

Yahoo chat group for people with Selective Sound Sensitivity:

Groups.yahoo.com/neo/groups/soundsensitivity/info

Self-Care for Calming the HSP Nervous System:

Books:

The Highly Sensitive Person's Companion by Ted Zeff

The Highly Sensitive Person's Survival Guide by Ted Zeff

The Highly Sensitive Person's Workbook by Elaine Aron

The Power of Sensitivity, chapter 18

Websites:

Psych Central article: "10 tips for HSPS":

psychcentral.com/blog/archives/2012/05/13/10-tips-for-highly-sensitive-people

Huffington Post article: "16 Habits of Highly Sensitive People":

www.huffingtonpost.com/2014/02/26/highly-sensitive-people-signs-habits_n_4810794.html

The HSP Healing CD with calming/grounding meditations and affirmations: drtedzeff.com/downloads

Sleep

Books:

The HSP Survival Guide by Ted Zeff, chapter 5

The Power of Sensitivity, chapter 19

Websites:

Tips to heal insomnia: drtedzeff.com/tips/insomnia

Somatic Healing

Books:

The Power of Sensitivity, chapter 20

Websites:

Authentic movement: authenticmovementcommunity.org

Bioenergetics: www.bioenergetic-therapy.com/index.php/en/

Hakomi: hakomiinstitute.com

Reiki healing: www.reiki.org

Rosen Method: www.rosenmethod.com

Somatic Experiencing: www.traumahealing.com

Spiritual Healing

Books:

The Power of Sensitivity, chapter 21

Websites:

Psychic/medium community: Cassadaga.org

Travel

Books:

The Power of Sensitivity, chapter 23

Websites:

Airplane seating charts: seatguru.com

Dealing with jet lag: www.antijetlag.com

References

Aron, Elaine. 2002. *The Highly Sensitive Child.* New York: Broadway Books.

———. 1996. *The Highly Sensitive Person.* New York: Carol Publishing.

———. 1999. *The Highly Sensitive Person's Workbook.* New York: Broadway Books.

———. 2010. *Psychotherapy and the Highly Sensitive Person: Improving Outcomes for That Minority of People Who Are the Majority of Clients.* New York: Routledge.

Belden, Rick, 1990. *Iron Man Family Outing: Poems About Transition Into A More Conscious Manhood.* Richard M. Belden.

Jaeger, Barrie, 2005. *Making Work Work for the Highly Sensitive Person.* New York: McGraw-Hill.

Kindlon, Dan and Michael Thompson. 2000. *Raising Cain.* New York: Ballantine.

Lad, Usha and Vasant. 1997. *Ayurvedic Cooking for Self-Healing.* New Mexico: Ayurvedic Press.

Morningstar, Amadea. 1995. *Ayurvedic Cooking for Westerners.* Wisconsin: Lotus Press.

Pollack, William. 1998. *Real Boys.* New York: Random House.

Zeff, Ted. 2007. *The Highly Sensitive Person's Companion.* Oakland, CA: New Harbinger Publications.

———. 2004. *The Highly Sensitive Person's Survival Guide.* Oakland, CA: New Harbinger Publications.

———. 2110. *The Strong Sensitive Boy.* San Ramon, CA: Prana Publishing.

CPSIA information can be obtained at www.ICGtesting.com
Printed in the USA
LVOW04s1321080215

426174LV00031B/1293/P